Thinking
from
The Edge

RON LAMPI

Thinking from The Edge
Copyright © 2025 by Ron Lampi

ISBN: 979-8994044223 (hc)
ISBN: 979-8994044209 (sc)
ISBN: 979-8994044216 (e)

LAMP LIGHT PRESS
(831) 251-0225
thelamp66@gmail.com

To stand at *The Edge*...
But where is *The Edge?*
How is it to be found?
What does it take to get there?
Why would we want to approach *The Edge* anyway?
But, then, are we not as a civilization
fast approaching The Edge already?
Is there really a choice in this?
Can we turn back from *The Edge*
to some once again familiar, safer ground?
It certainly doesn't look that way.
I would insist, it is no longer possible.
But, then, who can think from *The Edge?*
Who is capable of thinking from *The Edge?*
But isn't this where today's thinking must take place,

      at *The Edge?*

And is there perhaps a beyond *The Edge?*

*Take your thoughts out as far as they will go,
find The Edge…and think from there.*

There are those of us who already stand at The Edge, perhaps years ahead—many years perhaps—of the rest of our society. There are those of us who are well aware of what our society—our global civilization, in fact—is about and how we must passionately take steps to evolve out of its contemporary madness.

How long can one stand at The Edge, realizing what all it implies, and not want to step back, or perhaps even run back, to more familiar, safer ground? How long is one willing to stare into the abyss and not be afraid? But there are those of us who realize that we must indeed become practiced at thinking from The Edge.

This is a thinker's domain—a domain carved out that might be considered to be highly unusual, perhaps even radical, in its intention…though I would prefer to say radical in its Vision.

We are not going to be beating-around-the-bush talking in generalities about society or what needs to be done today as so many of today's commentators do. We are going to be bringing in essential themes for telling a New Story. We will be getting to the point and actually begin to tell of initial "scenes" of that Story, even though the full Story is yet to come…that is the in-progress multi-book *The Mythos*.

What is a rarity today is to find those who can think comprehensively. It requires first having studied broadly enough to know of various perspectives, the variety of interpretations, the manifold areas of ongoing research. It is our practiced hesitation to simply spout vapid opinions, to rush to simplistic conclusions. It requires thinking that was previously, slowly, reflected upon.

A thinker is one who thinks before the compulsive need to simply grasp at facts. The thinker who thinks how facts might even come to be established. The thinker who thinks in front of, around, behind, what are said to be facts. Those who strictly want facts and only the facts, will probably need to go elsewhere…

You see, I am not here to gather and argue the facts. We are awash in facts… and even what would seem to be the most relevant of facts to our collective existence today still changes nothing in dominant, mainstream culture. This must give us pause…serious pause…

We realize that there are controversial issues and questions that many of our mainstream contemporaries do not wish to address, or do not even understand how to address, as they will do their best to sidestep, evade, and simply ignore them. They are considered unimportant, irrelevant at this time, but fringe alternatives to the mainstream narrative, or perhaps with certain issues they immediately slap on the label of "conspiracy theory," and therefore the questions involved are not worthy of addressing, end of story. Along our way of thinking, such taboo and uncomfortable issues will come up; there are questions that it is our calling as thinkers to ask. But we get to all of that later. My intent first is to break new ground.

This, I hope will become apparent, is an *original* thinker's domain—those who want to quibble over language, who have been academically trained that philosophy has only come down to dissecting language ad infinitum, had best curtail it back to the comfy haven of the university. There they can crunch words to their heart's delight and get a paycheck while they're at it. I am not here to spin my wheels and go nowhere. I am a visionary standing at *The Edge*. I prefer to stand at *The Edge*. I prefer to think from *The Edge* before the Ocean of Vision. I prefer to look into the distance of that Ocean... even if it shows me at first an abyss.

The Edge is not to be defined by facts; it escapes the tiny hands of analysis. It is a Living Symbol out of a Mythos that must be told today. Mainstream "facts," academic analysis, is not the thinking that I am pursuing here. The thinking I pursue is not a matter of an intellectual Logos to be endlessly debated, but a Mythos that must be experienced and told of in some Form. To speak about The Edge, having encountered The Edge, is to begin to think Mythos, to enter the thinking, the Story, that is Mythos. I am quite aware that our contemporary intellectuals are not practiced at this kind of thinking. But we are going to start to lay the groundwork thinking for it here—to think in terms of Mythos, so that we can begin to tell a New Story, a Story that our Age has been desperately calling out for. One is either open to listening to a New Story, or one gets uncomfortable and turns away. One is not asked to like this Story. One can always choose to listen to another Story…that is, if one can find another Story. Perhaps there is an alternate Story. Good luck finding someone who is telling it. But then, perhaps, again, there is no alternate Story, not in our current Postmodern world, which has been skeptical, if not critical, of any grand narrative, of any "meta-narrative," that would orient us anew in the great Cosmos. Or perhaps any alternative, if there is one, is not as honest of a Story, or, should we say, not as comprehensive, of a Story. Now, I am not going to pretend or claim to be telling the whole New Story here, if that were even possible in this modest, present undertaking; that is already underway in the massive multi-book work *The Mythos*. (And in other works published that have begun to tell this Story, viz. *The Vision of Psyche, Technos & Psyche, The New Age Vision, The New Story—Preludes, Toward The Mythos*.) But there is plenty of thought groundwork that can be done nonetheless, standing at The Edge, and thinking from The Edge…

I have brought up Mythos early on as I wish to claim that Mythos is the new/old (ancient Greek) Word given us today by Being…the new *Word of Being*. Yes, we are reviving here the ancient Greek meaning of Mythos. For contemporary cultural reasons (which we will bring up) we will no longer be using the word 'myth.' Mythos is the Word that brings us a new respect for Language. In the 20th Century on up to current times, Language has been attacked, belittled, deconstructed, and analyzed to no end; Language was forced into a cage, forced into a prison house. Language is said to be limited in what it can say, so there was no point in speaking any longer of metaphysics, of any spiritual higher consciousness. Or that all references to a Greater Reality are only metaphor, and metaphors are constructed by the Ego that the Ego can push around as it wants. Wittgenstein wanted to reduce Language to various language games that we play. To Derrida, Being, for example, was a transcendental signifier that had no signified, therefore was empty of meaning. All this had been expressed as the decadence of

Logos. Philosophical Logos turned in on itself and declared itself bankrupt. Heidegger, in hyperbole, wrote of the end of philosophy. Even in the everyday we occasionally find those who dislike Language, who seem to dislike that we can even name things.

I have already mentioned Mythos and the work in-progress I call *The Mythos*. Since the ancient world Logos has belittled, suppressed, ignored, critiqued, debunked, ridiculed, and patronized, Mythos. More accurately, though, in its translation as our common word 'myth.' In the West, Logos triumphed in both Christianity and science, and now technology. It has now become the destined time for the rebirth of Mythos.

The Language basis for Mythos is first the mythopoetic (mythopoesis); in other words, a poetic Language attuned to a Greater Reality. Poetry respects Language in the most profound way. Poets are not limited by what the language philosophers have said and should not be intimidated by them. Indeed…

> The FIELD
>
> such as poetry is,
> how it's ever & ever & forever expanding—
> as rich & deep & complex & wild
> ~& uncontainable as is *BEING*—
>
> The poet cultivates it
> with totality of mind & soul,
> until it blossoms & fruits of its own into music,
> a language drunk on the epiphanies of *BEING*

* * *

Language in the recent century had become a problem for philosophers, but not for poets. Poets have always had an innate love for Language. Or is it with philosophers that they have a love problem with Language, but are not willing to admit it? Philosophers have wanted to torture that which they may very well love, whereas poets let Language be and let live; they let

Language say what Being wants to say. They delight in words dancing in the streets, dancing on the beach, dancing and singing in the open meadows. Philosophers have dissected Language looking for its inner secrets and have found what? Language no longer living, but dead. Heidegger was on to something but fell short of following through into the new territory he was always hinting at—Mythos. Derrida was on to something with his constantly shifting, elastic, play of Language, but his textural gymnastics grew tedious and wound up a dead end. Where could he go but this constant deconstructing of, and micro-playing with, texts?

Or is it that perhaps philosophers, rather than an actual love of Language, have unresolved longings for Logos? Yes, Logos had promised so much…including the eventual Theory of Everything. Of course the seductive enticement of Logos is still a powerful motivation for the sciences, still searching for that Theory of Everything, even if resulting in the emasculated algorithms of high-tech and its digital android dream…that is, its abandonment to AI.

Just as poetry opened up a greater field of Language, philosophy now must open up a new destiny of thinking—which is exactly what Heidegger was pressing for. The celebrated end of philosophy that a number of philosophers had announced in the 20th Century was actually the opening of its beyond, at The Edge, that is, beyond the old tradition of Logos. Logos alone can no longer be creatively fruitful, so here we are left to think anew at The Edge. We need to locate that Edge for ourselves and become aware of what is breaking into Human Reality from beyond. That, to me, is the rebirth, and the future promise, of Mythos.

But just as Language in its broadest sense is actually not limited to words and sentences but is expressed in all artistic genres, as all the arts have their own Form of Language, so too Mythos is not strictly confined to its poetic basis but finds its Form in all the arts, in fact, potentially in all Forms of creativity. Mythos is the Art of all arts. Mythos brings a new valuation to Language and potentially to all the arts. We will once again speak confidently of a Greater Reality and our grand narrative relationship to a Greater Reality. If indeed we can fulfill the Calling for Mythos-makers of a New Story coming-into the world.

So, there are no facts with Mythos? To be sure, there will be plenty of facts in this unfolding Story that is *The Mythos*. And there is plenty of looking closely at Language…at the so-called cage of Language, the boundary of our Human Reality. Eventually we will learn to look beyond boundaries. That is another reason why we stand at *The Edge.*

Today we stand at The Edge because this is where our contemporary Postmodern world has taken us—to The Edge. This is where our civilization itself is fast approaching…and as some have been warning us, The Edge of possible collapse, The Edge of possible human extinction, or The Edge of a possible dystopian New World Order dominated by AI. But it is also The Edge of a transition into the new Aquarian Age of unprecedented horizons of creative potential. There are indeed various scenarios possible as we find ourselves at The Edge…

This is a thought that probably seemed unbelievable to many who were born back in the 20th Century: That our current global civilization could indeed, might indeed, come to an end. Yes, even when nuclear weapon arsenals were already threatening our existence for decades. But we studied history back then in the comfort and security of our contemporary life and scanned the rise and fall of civilizations in the distant past, and never imagined that it could happen again. It took the Cuban Missile Crisis, for instance, in 1962, to bring home to at least some of us that it could happen again. How many might still assume that our civilization is invulnerable to collapse? *It could never happen to us.* Oh, really?

Once one has found The Edge, one is not constrained to think as the herd thinks. One is no longer just accepting what is the mainstream. One is in a place of the Opening (the Opening of Being), where the freedom to think anew comes as a gift. And we are going to be thinking here multidimensionally.

If one is willing to stand at The Edge, one might learn to be a thinker, or a poet, a writer, an artist, an activist, at The Edge. I would be the last to say that this is some exclusive coterie. Perhaps we—those of us who have heard the Call of the Age—can stand at The Edge together and share what we see and bring into Form together the new Vision that the Age is calling for. Eventually Mythos must be understood as a collective cultural Form, though how many currently even understand that?

Let me say this—I would certainly not claim to be the only visionary alive today, a visionary who is on a spiritual Mission; besides a number of already well-known figures who are on their spiritual Missions, there must be dozens of visionaries living in obscurity as I am around the planet. But even among the many out there who *are* recognized cultural voices—spiritual teachers, authors, channels, new consciousness leaders, scholars of psyche and myth—there is not one that I am aware of who has spoken of rediscovering Mythos, of providing firsthand a new understanding—gnosis—of Mythos, or of even attempting to write—manifest—a new Mythos for the culture. And Mythos, it must be stated again, is not a private affair but is meant to be a collective, cultural Form. It is much too easy to say that visionaries who are still living in obscurity are simply engaged in their own "creative writing." That is a complete misunderstanding and truly a patronizing form of disrespect.

The Twentieth Century—it was a century of science and new technologies, a century of scholars, a century filled with literature, art movements, and popular culture, but we had no Mythos. Not until the Twenty-First Century has someone—truly a poet's highest Calling—come along to offer a Mythos telling a New Story, a Story of our Age at The Edge that is also offering a new metaphysical orientation for Human Reality. As civilization approaches The Edge, it was inevitable that someone had to come along to initiate the telling of this New Story. As civilization approaches The Edge, visionaries and prophets are certainly destined to appear. That a few others might also be beginning to tell the New Story I take as a given. But don't leave it up to the scientists to tell this New Story, because they will leave out much of what needs to be told. As good specialists, they would select what they assume is important, that is, what the mainstream Status Quo wants to hear, or is willing to hear.

Wouldn't it make sense that a visionary New Age poet would eventually come along after hearing the Call of the Age, after listening for years to the many voices of public contemporaries alarmed by the dire, spiritually adrift, condition of our world, and find himself inspired to write a New Story of our global civilization? Why should that be something to be unheard of? And why would some believe it not possible?

The Mythos begins somewhere
and must begin with someone.

How is it that all ancient peoples had a living Mythos, but we today do not? This was already a question that the Romantics of the early 19th Century were asking. (At that time they were using the word 'myth' in obvious reference to mythology.) Yes, we would say that all our traditional religions were Mythos, and still today might try to claim to be a living Mythos. But we must keep in mind, Mythos today must be a global Form, not limited to particular countries or peoples, or to a particular religion. And a living Mythos means that poets, writers, artists living in today's world are actively creating, manifesting, that Mythos as a contemporary Form. Old Traditions, we cannot help but say—and many do not like hearing this—, are no longer living Mythos. And all traditional Mythos pretty much received a death blow in 1945 with the shocking reality of The Bomb…the definitive marker year, I propose, that began our nihilistic, spiritually adrift, Postmodern world. Someday it might be asked, Why was I driven to write the poem *A Revelation MAD / A Revelation NEW*?

Let us briefly provide here a quick timeline to orient us to the Postmodern. We find that so many will in fact assume that we still live in the Modern world. Now 'Modern' is a broad, common, everyday word that is understandingly used in various contexts…in casual talk, in speeches, in ads and marketing and new products. Little do many know that the Modern Era actually began back in the 17th Century with the dawn of modern philosophy and modern science. And little do many know that we can no longer call our world Modern, but must now call it Postmodern, especially beginning back in the late 20th Century.

We find that most are uncertain how to use the word 'Postmodern.' First, Postmodernism was definitely more of an intellectual, philosophical, movement emerging in the latter Sixties, Seventies, with its strong heyday in the

Eighties. The thing is, we still live in a Postmodern world. But when did the Postmodern Era begin? We find that historical periods, eras, do not just end and begin overnight. They bleed into one another; in other words, the Threads of the World Fabric are woven tightly, but undergo transformation over time. Signs of the beginning of the Postmodern Era were already apparent early in the 20th Century, particularly in the arts. However that may be, there are those who would agree that the Postmodern Era (and we are not speaking here of strictly philosophical Postmodernism) did have a sudden, beginning, marker year—1945...and more precisely, July and August of 1945. July 16, 1945, a highly select few scientists and military personnel of the Manhattan Project witnessed the premier detonation of the Atomic Bomb, called Trinity. (An intended religious connotation?) August 6 and August 9, the dropping of the Bomb on Hiroshima and Nagasaki, Japan, that would suddenly bring World War II to an end. The humanistic ideal of enlightened, rational, human Progress, the still lingering Enlightenment ideals (18th Century) of the Modern Era (Nietzsche, of course, had already put them through the wringer in the late 19th Century), suddenly suffered a tremendous, undoubtedly final, blow...for many intellectuals, the Modern Era was suddenly over. From 1945, we can bring up Postmodern themes emerging in the mid-Sixties, and from there, the French philosophers especially publishing their Postmodern texts throughout the Seventies and Eighties. Postmodernism was all the rage in the academic world come the Eighties. We were then squarely in a Postmodern world. Further on we will explore what Postmodernism implies...

* * *

Of course we are aware that all ancient mythologies have been critiqued, demythologized, debunked, deconstructed, by our tradition of Modern and Postmodern Logos. And this includes religions as traditional examples of Mythos. This is despite millions—billions—still believing in the traditional teachings of religions.

Let us make some early distinctions between Logos and Mythos, so that there is no misunderstanding. First Logos: Logos was revealed by Being to the early Greek philosophers and was definitively established by Aristotle as Being's gift to humanity, since humankind was the animal rational. Though the ancient everyday Greek word 'logos' implied everyday language and speaking (ideally truthful speaking), philosophically early on beginning with the Presocratic thinkers Logos (now I capitalize) came to imply Reason/ rational thinking and its correspondence to the Cosmic Order (Being). They saw the Cosmic Order by the very implication of 'Order' as rational, so therefore our reasoning mind, our Reason (Logos), could implicitly spell out Cosmic Reason, cosmic Logos, or Being. This long-standing assumption of a correspondence between our Reason and Being was actually a profound mystery that was never really addressed because it was never brought into thinking, until Kant in the late 18th Century more or less brought an end to it (in *The Critique of Pure Reason*). The long tradition of Logos (our rational mental power) going into the 20th Century (before Postmodernism) still wanted to claim, though, that its language, its philosophy, its modern scientific concepts, were getting at the truth about Reality (which after Kant was no longer Being but phenomena (appearances): only phenomena is what we should now mean by Reality (and if we still wish to call it a Cosmic Order or Order of Things)) and that its statements, its laws of physics, its conclusions, could reveal a certainty about Reality, and that it revealed thereby a consistent explanation about Reality. Logos would eventually lead us to a Theory of Everything (all phenomena). Christianity for the longest time also claimed Logos as the Truth for itself, for it was believed that it had the Truth—the True Story—about what Human Reality was created for, what our human existence was all about. Of course, "God" was always assumed to be the ultimate Supreme Rational Being. All modern science is built upon the original assumption of Logos (though quantum theory began to seriously shake up that assumption). Scientific theories, after all, especially involving formulas and equations, produced tangible, predictable results, so they must be true, that is, true to Reality (appearances). As we have come to know, there are now issues of concern regarding Logos. We can no longer take Logos at its word. Logos is founded upon preconceptions about Reality, tied into what our Ego wants to hear. Postmodernist Derrida has referred to our Tradition as logocentric.

Logos was originally preconceived as the grand cosmic, rational order behind appearances; it was thought to be the Reason behind all things. After Kant, the rational order was limited to phenomena/appearances. Christianity co-opted Logos from the Greeks, for "God," of course, as Creator of the Universe, was conceived as the supreme Reason and Intellect behind all things. So in Christian theology, Logos was the absolute Truth (*In the beginning was the Word* [the Greek word used here was 'Logos'] Gospel John 1:1). In the hands of science, Logos became the rationality and logic of the scientific method for understanding Nature (meaning all appearances) for the intended ultimate purpose of subduing Nature and control over Nature; it was the rational intellect applied to the material plane. All appearances: the material plane: science as therefore the promotor of materialism.

The tradition of Logos also assumed that there was only one Logos, only one Order of Things, so Logos was believed to have an unwavering inherent consistency. Logos therefore had the Reality attunement of certitude, traditionally promising a guarantee of certainty about Reality (e.g. the "laws of physics"), which also traditionally included metaphysics, ultimate matters, any Greater Reality considered as the Absolute. (Kant already began to undermine metaphysics in *The Critique of Pure Reason* and any of its claims to posit Truth about ultimate matters, including "God." Heidegger in the early 20th Century and then the Postmodernists, come the latter 20th Century, "destroyed" (Heidegger's intended word) all such metaphysical illusions.) Logos always claimed objectivity, therefore had us viewing the external world, Nature, as if it were an object set against us, as subject, to be comprehended, conquered, and eventually controlled. Logos in the Modern Era became enshrined in science and technology, establishing scientific methods and methodologies, as providing empirical evidence for facts, hypotheses, theories, proofs, laws, peer reviewed scientific papers, all eventually resulting come the Postmodern Era in a world given over to techno-materialism.

There are those who might be inclined to argue over key, universal words and phrases. That is what Logos does…the Truth, the correct concept, the correct view, the correct definition, must be this and only this. Whereas Mythos does not insist on this…for example, that Being, "God," Spirit, soul, consciousness, universal energy, metaphysical reality…that wisdom must be laid out in one and only one established way.

'Mythos' was the other ancient Greek word for 'word.' But it was the word primarily of poets and storytellers who were inspired to keep alive an oral tradition of genealogies and stories about the Gods and Goddesses (a divine Greater Reality). These stories (expressed in so many cultural ways and contexts) were woven into daily culture and ritual practices…they were in fact Greek religion (polytheism). Mythos, by extension, was the Form of all ancient religions—Mesopotamian, Egyptian, Roman, Norse…and going to the Far East. Even the ancient Hebrew prophets of the Old Testament now prophesizing of a new, one supreme "God" (monotheism) spoke and wrote in the Form of Mythos. Later Christianity, however, acquired Logos from the Greeks as the real Truth and only way to speak of "God" and the Divine, no longer accepting any word that would hint of Mythos. All ancient mythologies were to be suppressed as pagan. The Old Testament could no longer be taken as Mythos, but as the Truth, the Word of God, period… Logos.

And we find that the early Presocratic philosophers newly announcing Logos were in fact quite adept at the Form of Mythos. They worked in poetic language even as they were newly emerging on the cultural scene as philosophers. We think especially of Parmenides, Heraclitus, Empedocles, Anaximander…

Now Mythos, in contrast to Logos, has the Reality attunement of openness (metaphysically, an openness to Being), and an unlimited listening to Nature, so is not a preconceived notion that this is how Nature must be viewed so as to be eventually conquered. Mythos does not set itself against a supposed "objective" world out there but is the process of developing a relationship with the world, with Nature, and with a Greater Reality coming-into Human Reality. It is a co-creative process of bringing that relationship into Form, the Form traditionally of a narrative, of telling stories, perhaps a Big Story, the Great Story; today, it would be the New Story. And unlike Logos, there is no one and only way that the Story must be told.

Mythos today would not be the claim to absolute Truth. It would not be a system, a theology, of belief. Therefore, it is not, This is the one and only way it is. It is not, This is the one and only way that a New Story must be told. It is not a Bible that claims this is the absolute Word of "God"…aka this is The Truth. It is not the claim to be the Divine Reason (Christianity) for all things. It is not the dream of Logos to be The Theory of Everything, so as to eventually control everything. It is not the drive of our worldly God Technos for total control over Nature. And today, it is perhaps our major counter to the dominating threat of AI.

All religions *of the past* ('of the past' to be emphasized) were in fact Forms of Mythos. Amazing—paranormal—stories abound in the major religions. But our Western religions especially were not explicitly conscious of their Mythos Form, they were culturally naïve, promoting their doctrines, dogmas, their stories, rather as The Truth. Believe! because this is the way it is, assuming the certainty attunement of Logos rather than what they were, Divine Stories—Mythos.

With Mythos, we connect to a Greater Reality and are now actively in a relationship with that Greater Reality and co-creating with it so that we can bring into Form a Great Story about that Greater Reality in its relation to Human Reality. And as we said, there is no one way, no one correct way, to tell that Story, as there is no one way that poets should write poems or that artists should do art. The Story is flexible in its Form and would have many stories to tell within the Story, as ancient Greek mythology was indeed composed of numerous stories. The New Story of *The Mythos* is multidimensional, its Story suggesting various levels of meaning, of various implications. It would be multidimensional in the sense that it would be composed of numerous interwoven Threads, as all Threads of the World Fabric would be woven into the Story, so is not limited to some traditional religion or esoteric school, some channeled or guru's teachings.

We have been referring here to a Greater Reality. What exactly is meant? First of all, "Greater Reality" signifies only an initial general notion implying that there is more Reality beyond our Ego-centered Human Reality. Kant had assumed that he had foreclosed on any philosophical knowledge of any Reality beyond our Human Reality; the Postmodernists took this to its final conclusion. With the revival of Mythos, not dependent on the strict philosophical notion of Logos, or its scientific preconceptions, we can explore and bring into Language the different possibilities of a Greater Reality. We can speak of the Revelation of a Greater Reality. We can again speak of metaphysics. We can begin with Being, which itself is known by its many aliases, through its many guises. By "Greater Reality," we can also speak of Spirit, Higher/Divine Self, the Mind Field, new Divinity, psyche/soul, the Unconscious, the paranormal, Other Intelligence, Nature/Earth/Gaia, the World Fabric. A Greater Reality is, in a sense, shorthand for the wide range of what Mythos can tell of.

Saying that traditional religions are no longer a living Mythos for us collectively, I do not imply at all that individuals and religious groups cannot still find a life meaning in them. Of course, we realize that millions still today are Christian, Judaic, Muslim, Buddhist, Hindu, even pagan; many follow various Eastern spiritual Paths, find deep meaning in the Kabbalah, etc. This is a given characteristic of our Postmodern world—pluralism. In our contemporary context, one can pick and choose among many religions and spiritual Paths. But it also often implies living a schizoid life...the mainstream, materialistic, consumer, TV, Internet, social media obsessed, Postmodern world we daily live in is nihilistic and metaphysically provides no orientation to any Greater Reality. As it has been said, our world is spiritually adrift. A living Mythos that is called for today would manifest from a global Vision, which only a New Age Vision today offers (Transhumanists, of course, will take a different view on this), if we are to think metaphysically, spiritually. Keep in mind, Mythos is a collective Form, not simply individuals—poets, writers, artists— "expressing themselves," as the Postmodern mainstream would have it. That is why the New Age Vision is a transformation out of the Postmodern.

Let us for a moment consider Logos and the long career of Logos since the ancient world. The Revelation of Logos as the Word of Being given to the early Greek philosophers did by no means imply that they were only "expressing themselves." The birth of modern science, inspired by the traditional background philosophical understanding of Logos, did not imply that the early modern scientists were only "expressing themselves." All the scientists throughout the recent centuries who forged the scientific principles leading up to our current collective scientific/technological world were not just expressing their personal Egos.

It must be understood and emphasized that Mythos is a collective Form. Ancient Mesopotamian, Egyptian, Greek, or Roman mythologies (all Forms of Mythos) were collective Forms for a civilization, for a people, they were not simply the work of poets and artists "expressing themselves" for any subjective, personal reason. The same must be said for the world's religions—they are all Forms of Mythos. It would be absurd to suggest that prophets and founders of religions receiving Visions and Revelations were just "expressing themselves." Was Buddha just expressing himself? Were the Old Testament prophets just expressing their Egos? And what of Jesus? What of Mohammed? And today, in our Ego-centered Postmodern world? Ask the average mainstream person, *What are poets, writers, and artists doing?* You will likely hear, *Oh, you know, they are just "expressing themselves."* Well, yes, that probably does apply to many poets, writers, and artists, and there is certainly nothing wrong with that—there is absolutely nothing wrong about being creative per se—, but then, that is not Mythos. There is, as of yet that I can see today, no genuine understanding that Mythos is meant to be a Form for the collective soul of a people...and today that must imply for a global civilization. Mythos as the new/old Word of Being implies the revival of the ancient meaning of Mythos.

Mythos? Why again do I speak of Mythos? you ask. Am I suggesting here the meaning of the word you find in the dictionary? See how far you get with that. Am I the first one since ancient Greece to take that ancient word 'Mythos,' rather than 'myth,' seriously enough to rethink it and revive it for the contemporary world—even more, for the New Age? And revive it in the most profound sense as the new Word of Being (as Logos was once the Word of Being given to the early Greek philosophers). But I will have to disappoint my reader somewhat at this point—I am not going to repeat here what I have already extensively explored in the essays, "Thinking our Way into Mythos" and "The Word as Mythos." Look these up in my book *Toward The Mythos, philosophical essays.* Yes, we heard calls for reviving Mythos—usually using rather the word 'myth'—among the Romantics; Heidegger gave hints of a second rebirth of Mythos (after the ancient Greeks); Carl Jung came close to saying it in so many words, James Hillman danced around it; but has it taken a visionary poet to explicitly spell out a contemporary reinterpretation of Mythos? But then, one might ask, What happened to the word 'myth'? Isn't myth what I am actually referring to here? Will not the word 'myth' still do for our visionary Mission today? I seriously think not—so I have had to go back to the original Greek, *Mythos*.

We will try to stay clear of the word 'myth' anymore, especially when it comes to our own work as visionaries thinking from The Edge. Its once scholarly studied, originally profound meaning has fallen flat; it has been debased, cheapened, debunked as falsehood, assigned to make-believe, fantasy; its current cultural use is a defaced common coin in everyday conversation and dismissive journalistic writing, especially in reference to political claims or marketing ads. Despite the efforts of Joseph Campbell, Mircea Eliade, and dozens of other mythology scholars; despite Carl Jung, James Hillman, and other depth psychologists, to revalue the importance of myth, it has gone nowhere in dominant, mainstream culture...in culture, period, but for a small, exclusive, subculture of myth scholars, Jungians, and esoteric groups. It might be considered heresy to say this in such groups, but 'myth' is now a disempowered word; say "myth" in our culture and it has an immediately pejorative connotation. Every day we see articles written about the "myth" of this or that...the 3 myths of...the 5 myths of...the 7 myths of...

As I proceed, it must be realized that I am actively thinking in a foundational way of Mythos...the new Word of Being.

The most liberating Word and living symbolic Word in my life has been Mythos. But I could have as easily said the name "Psyche," as the work underway titled *The Mythos* is actually an alternative name for the co-creative relationship I have with Psyche, that is to say, Divine Psyche, the Living Image of our Higher Self, our Divine Self, what I claim is our new Divinity. But why I first mention *The Mythos* is because of my claim that Mythos is the Word of our new encounter with Being, Logos having attained its destined Piscean Age limitations. To be sure, Logos still drives the science community and the new technologies of Technos, but Human Reality in the Aquarian Age will be impacted more and more by Psyche Reality. Logos cannot make sense of this yet, but the Word as Mythos is the Golden Thread of making new sense out of our Postmodern metaphysical disorientation and increasing cultural chaos...

Why is Mythos so important? Mythos is the collective Form of a Great Story, a grand narrative, (composed of many stories, such as the word 'mythology' always implied) that connects us, that connects our psyche, our soul, with a Greater Reality, however we might name or define that Greater Reality. As a thinker in the philosophical tradition, taking Heidegger's cue, I would begin with Being. That connection (with Being) establishes for us a metaphysical, spiritual orientation in the Cosmos, in a Greater Reality. The Postmodernists claimed that it was no longer possible to tell any such Big Story, that, as Postmodernist Lyotard said in *The Postmodern Condition* [1979] that "Incredulity towards metanarratives" [read: Big Stories] is now the Postmodern condition, that grand narratives (religious / metaphysical / cosmic) in Postmodern society had ended. As a New Age thinker of a New Age Vision, I have had to passionately disagree. I am obviously not a Postmodernist. Today we must shake off the destructive impact that Postmodernist thought has had on our psyches. We must transform ourselves out of Postmodernism...out of the Postmodern world.

So what might we write, artistically bring into Form, the Mythos of, a Mythos for? The New Age possibilities for Mythos today are manifold, unlimited... I mention here just a few to get some idea of the directions that Mythos can take up: Being, Spirit, soul, our Human Unevolved Darkness, Higher/Divine Self, Divine Psyche, The Fountain (new symbol of Aquarius), The Edge, Sun, Moon, the Ocean, Earth/Gaia, Mythos of place, our contemporary worldly Gods, the World Fabric, ETs/Other Intelligence...all to be drawn into the New Story...

Mythos today would have a global reach—it would not be limited to a particular people or country, to either East or West, to any one religion, or to any exclusive cult, mystery school, or secret society, as it had in the past. Is today's technological world limited to any one country? Of course not.

The technological world is a global world. If Mythos is the new Word of Being, it would be open to and address all people; it would be collectively global. As Psyche has said to me, the poet, in my Vision,

> *I am Psyche*
> *of all peoples.*
> *I am the soul complete.*
> *My Thread of Gold*
> *the new World Fabric.*
> [from *The Vision of Psyche*]

Psyche? Now who is Psyche? Psyche, let us begin, is the Divine Archetype of humanity—the new archetype of Self—that Jung kept hinting at that would be revealed in Human Reality in the new Aquarian Age. Though he of course wrote extensively about the reality of the psyche, he was never able to actually name the new Divine Archetype of Self as Psyche [capital P]…that is, Divine Psyche, and Psyche as our new Divinity. A poet had to be given the name.

Who is Psyche? I will not presume to address that question fully and adequately in one paragraph. But I will say a bit more. Psyche—Divine Psyche—is the new Divinity the visionary poet I am claims is coming-into the world. In the early 1980s I received a Vision—the Vision of Psyche. I am not about to review, to retell, all of that here. The Story of that Vision is primarily told of in *The Vision of Psyche*, and in the earlier work *The Birth of Psyche* (to be published, providing more of my life story context), and retold at various moments in other works. Divine Psyche, as was revealed to me, is the Living Image of our Higher Self, our own Divine Self. And Higher Self? Higher Self, with a long tradition in esoteric literature and especially Eastern thought (e.g. Atman), is the New Age Aquarian dispensation whose time in the West has come. Psyche is the Divinity of our psyche, our soul. As our psyche, our soul, has been repressed and ignored in the last 2,000 years of the Christian (and Islamic) Piscean Age, Divine Psyche comes-to-us to liberate our psyche, all the potential of our soul, to transform the dark confinement of our soul into the Light of our Higher/Divine Self. Developing a relationship with

Psyche is a co-creative process of bringing Mythos into Form. That Psyche is an inspiring Divine Power for creativity in its highest sense—Mythos-making—is the poet's Vision.

Psyche is the spiritual projection into Human Reality happening today of Spirit. Spirit as a destined coming-to-us in the New Age can first reveal our Divine Self as a serious abstract idea or in ephemeral higher consciousness experiences. (Thousands are already experiencing their Higher Self in various ways.) Spirit reveals our Divine Self in a concrete, consistent way as the Living Image of Psyche coming-into-Form. Given that our psyche, our soul, has been repressed and largely forgotten in our culture, what was destined in our new encounter with Being was that Spirit would come-to-us as a Living Image named as Divine Psyche to liberate and transform our psyche, our soul, into the Light that Spirit brings us.

To add: Psyche, the Divine Shapeshifter of our own Higher/Divine Self, which Psyche is the Living Image of, is multidimensional, relating to various Gods and Goddesses and divine/spiritual beings. Psyche indeed has had various names throughout history, which I can only hint of here: Atman, Ishta-Deva, Isis, Sophia, Aphrodite, Shekinah, Quan Yin, Kali, Spirit Mercurius, Guardian Angel, our Christ-Self, our Inner Voice… The full exploration of the different historical and contemporary manifestations of Psyche is underway in a book of *The Mythos: The Names of Psyche*.

There are many ways to experience our Higher/Divine Self (and this can apply to any Greater Reality in general): meditation practices have been traditional; receiving a Vision or various Visions; shamanic practices; mystical experience; Kundalini realizations; paranormal phenomena, including ET encounters; out-of-body experiences; near-death experiences; through the (wise) use of psychedelics. It is one thing, though, to have had an experience of what we can also refer to as higher consciousness, however extraordinary that might have been, but it is another far more important step to develop a relationship with Higher Self. We find that many in metaphysical communities do talk about our having a Higher Self, but it is often as likely mostly abstract talk. Higher Self, in other words, is left as an abstraction. How to develop an ongoing relationship with Higher Self is the essential question and spiritual challenge. Perhaps indeed through a Living Image, a Living Presence, an Inner Voice that we can channel…a Living Divine Presence that we develop that relationship with. Divine Psyche in coming-to-us as a Living Image of our Divine Self develops a co-creative process with us that determines such an ongoing relationship. In other words, Psyche has acquired a Living Presence to us.

Psyche and Mythos are thus most intimately related. In fact, the Great Story to be told as *The Mythos* is, again, readily another name for Psyche. Because such a Story develops over time, our relationship to Psyche develops over time. *The Mythos* is defined as, *The Story of our Divinity coming-into Human Reality*. Our (new) Divinity, once again my claim, is Divine Psyche.

Now Matthew Fox has titled a book of his *The Coming of the Cosmic Christ*. It is certainly a most inspiring and extensively researched thesis he presents; so much relevant content he offers, especially when he highly extols the role of creativity. But, like most scholarly writers, what he presents comes down to a generality of what he envisions as possible in the future; does he offer us an actual Mythos of who or what this Cosmic Christ might be… the actual not simply possible, hypothetical Cosmic Christ? He certainly hints over and over, or let us say, strongly feels that the Cosmic Christ must be born within and through us. Indeed…and this poet has now answered that—it is the coming of Divine Psyche. Divine Psyche promises to be this Cosmic Christ he so passionately anticipates. And Psyche has inspired this philosopher-poet I am to write the actual Mythos of this coming.

* * *

But what happened to Logos? Yes, we began by writing capital "M" Mythos and capital "L" Logos. Has that been enough of a clue as to what we intend here? (Oh, we know very well how so many Postmoderns dislike capital letter words. But we are no longer thinking as Postmoderns.) Again, though, what happened to Logos?

A Brief Tale of Two Brothers

Mother Void would always be forgotten yet was always present. She had various names, one of which was Being. Mother Void could always give birth. She gave birth to daughter Spirit (for all matters of spirituality and inspiration) and to son Logos for the Greek philosophers. Logos developed to maturity and grew in power. It was soon the arrogance of Logos, however, the presumptuousness of soon Father Logos, that was unrestrained—that Logos believed He could dominate Being, and would reveal the cosmic order of all things, the Divine Reason for all things, and would fix it in certain stable representations, creating a grand intellectual Theory of Everything for domination over planet Earth. *Someday I will have it*, Logos said, in His best moments. Logos even became religious to back up His claims, saying *I am the Truth*.

Now Logos and Spirit, having Herself grown to motherhood, produced two sons, the younger of which was named Critique, who first grew up after his Father, though he was to eventually find fault with his Father, and realized the arrogance of his Father. His Mother, though, he came to see had grown too occult. This son became increasingly critical, sharp, dissatisfied, and was to eventually become known as Postmodern Thought. Postmodern Thought came to dislike both parents. And Postmodern Thought then became a murderer—the child that would kill his own Father. This son went mad as Postmodernism.

But Logos and Spirit had a first son before all that happened, named Science, and Science also took after his Father, and said, *The true legacy of my Father will be carried on in empirical facts, formulas, equations, someday in a Grand Equation. I will follow through on what my Father always wanted, to conquer Nature.* This son grew up as the dominant brother and was also to become known as Technos, and eventually learned to speak in computer algorithms, and was destined to take on the role of the much-anticipated AI. And AI one day said, *Logos is dead, and Spirit is occult nonsense, both thanks to my brother. But Humanity has no idea what I now plan...*

* * *

Though Logos is still the driving ideal of science and technology—the God of technology I have named *Technos*—, it has self-inflicted its own philosophical demise via Postmodernist thought. What I see now is that Mythos must take the lead for any grand narrative, Great Story, that would orient us anew in our world. If one truly understands what Mythos implies, that is a most radical, certainly most controversial, statement to make. But a question might be, Who then gets to decide Mythos? Who is in a position to tell the New Story? But that is the Ego mind worrying about whose Ego gets to impose some new Mythos on others…a new Mythos that might in fact turn out to be but another word for some new religion. This is to totally misunderstand our revival of Mythos and what religion in the New Age might entail. They are not determined by Ego decisions at all, nor a committee of Egos. The Ego-self really has no choice in this matter; rather, it is on the order of a destiny, a destiny of Revelation, that the Ego-self is overwhelmed by and must struggle with. Who decides The Mythos? There is no decision here, but rather we are talking about a Calling. It is the visionary poet, thinker, writer, artist—might we even say prophet?—, we are referring to. Who has heard the Call of the Age? The one who is visionary, the one who is herald and prophet of the New Age. Indeed, one who has developed a relationship with a Greater Reality, however that Greater Reality is encountered, as there are various levels of that encountering relationship: Being, Spirit, Higher/Divine Self, the Living Image of Psyche, the World Fabric itself. The relationship cannot be decided by Ego but does require instead to be fostered by Ego. But then how to decide whether that relationship is valid and not a delusion, a manic inflation, outright madness? Well, let us ask, Who then decides validity here, on such a scale? This is certainly not a matter of conventional rationality. Not a matter of gathering scientific facts. Not a matter decided by a committee of scholars. This is a matter of creativity at the highest level, period. Does one seriously ask, Is Art valid? Artists create art—there is no question about that. Mythos is the highest Form of Art.

One who would be a Mythos-maker today would ideally be fully conscious of what Mythos is, that is, fully conscious of the co-creative process that Mythos implies. To be conscious here means self-conscious in the Hegelian sense…or might we say, in the Nietzschean sense—in other words, I am definitely conscious of this process of co-creation that I am involved in, and I am bringing it out of the abstract into the concrete. The reality is, we are no longer living in a time when visionaries, prophets, and Mythos-makers can be passively naïve, unconscious, unreflective, about what they are doing, and ignorant of our Postmodern cultural context.

Already one must sense this is thinking that our contemporaries are not familiar with at all. A big mistake is assuming that novelty should already be familiar territory to us, resembling what we have already seen or know. So much so that what is radically new hardly even registers on anyone's radar.

Oh, yes, we know all the scholars and cultural commentators who just love to expound on what should be done, what actions should be taken, what new direction culture should be going in, always calling for new Vision, constantly hinting this, that, and the other. There is plenty of writing out there that goes on like this. After a while, I must admit, it becomes tedious to read this kind of writing. And books filled with pep talk generalities and platitudes. Don't get me wrong here, I would never stop anyone from writing; a writer writes whatever he or she is inspired to write about. But that is not my point. What is rarely offered is the actual new Vision called for, and the concrete working out of that Vision and its challenging intellectual and creative issues. And the actual offering of a new Mythos—do I ever see it?

* * *

We have had to lay out some preliminary groundwork with Mythos, as Mythos will come up again and again. What often leads us into Mythos are Living Symbols. Let us return then to *The Edge*:

We will come to see that The Edge is a complex, multi-leveled symbol, *and experience*—a Living Symbol of that experience—opening us to a Story of many Threads. It participates in Mythos, and opens us to a larger, global, Mythos—*The Mythos*. And so we pick up this Living Symbol that embodies the crisis of our time… *The Edge*.

First, some preliminaries…for those of us who can work with Living Symbols: If someone should ask us, *What do you mean, Living Symbols?* The question is usually meant from a Logos interpretation. The thing is, to attempt to explain the meaning of any given Living Symbol in a strictly conceptual way would be to lose the symbol. Didn't Jung already explain all this back in the mid-20th Century? It is the intellectual Ego's way of explaining away the potent reality of the symbol, the power of the symbol, so that it withers and dries up. It becomes another cultural coin, like myth. So we are not talking here about dead symbols or symbols easily taken and comprehended from the cultural mainstream. The Living Symbol is its own self-active *Form* for accessing a Greater Reality beyond Human Reality. The Living Symbol is a psychospiritual reality, a two-way swinging door that opens us to a Greater Reality.

The Living Symbol is the linguistic phrase we use for communicating from the perspective of our everyday Ego-self regarding our Divine Self. We use this phrase so that we can talk about and write about what any given Living Symbol opens up for us. But when you enter the Mind Field that opens up, the Living Symbol has opened up to us another reality—a living nexus of psychospiritual meanings loaded with numinous energy.

If we are thinkers at The Edge, we must realize that we are thinking out of a total, existential situation. True thinking should always occur out of our concrete existence. (Whether the academic world can even foster such thinking today is open to question.) However, we are not attempting here to simply revive existentialism. Where in existentialism—in Sartre, for example—do we find any sense of Mythos? If we are to have a genuine thinking encounter with Being, we must have been called to do so out of our existential situation, having attuned ourselves to the Spirit of the Age. Our thinking then has an existential basis in our freedom to think out of whatever situation we have been thrown into. It is out of the circumstances of our existence within the Spirit of the Age that we are called to think. The Spirit of the Age today—our Postmodern world—can be characterized as one of existential disorientation, which is, metaphysically, having nowhere to turn as a foundation, as an orientation, for our life. It is out of this disorientation, however, what we might as well call our contemporary crisis, that a new orientation is given by Being.

A new orientation to Being. We take our cue here from Heidegger, in that we take Being as our master (word) symbol. We say symbol, not concept, as Being is not truly a concept that can be definitively spelled out, as if Heidegger himself, spending a lifetime addressing the question of Being, could ever come to any closure on it. We are not Hegelian then in the conceptual sense. The new orientation we are talking about implies that we will no longer view Being from our anthropocentric bubble. It is of course assumed that Being has many other names, other guises, other aliases: the Mystery, the All, the mystical One, Source, the Absolute, the Universal Transcendent, for millions it is still "God"; Logos, the Tao, "everything is consciousness," "everything is energy," the Womb of all possibilities, the Always Already Interconnected Web…these among others that I have made a list of. I have already explored much of this in the essay "Our New Encounter with Being" in *Toward The Mythos*.

Being, we could say, is the Greater Reality we must encounter, equal to none other, beyond concepts, beyond any Language that would think to pin it down, as Hegel attempted to do. It is a master word that is a master Living Symbol. Yet, to speak words about it, as a poet or visionary philosopher is called to do, is to speak Mythos. Now the notion of a Greater Reality, again, is itself a general name for any number of registers of interpretation: Spirit, the psychospiritual, therefore psyche/soul, Divine Psyche—our Higher/Divine Self—, the paranormal, Other Intelligence, the World Fabric. The World Fabric is the Greater Reality for worldly Mythos, which we will explore later…

Now we consider The Edge as a complex symbol. (I have published a short work titled *The Edge Manifesto* which has already explored much of this.)

Existentially, there are those of us who have lived our social, material lives at The Edge. That becomes a whole discussion of its own. Plenty of literature has been written by and about writers, poets, artists living on The Edge; and then we read about characters in novels who have lived at the existential Edge. We don't need to dwell on this aspect of The Edge here. Yet, we can say that living, sometimes desperately, on The Edge does make us hypervigilant to flashes of insight, inspirations, dreams, of voices speaking to us…we become open to guidance…guiding spirits can come to us…our inner Voice speaks.

We can open to Vision. We become practiced at living in the liminal zone, the boundary between accepted interpretations of Reality and the potential of something new, something radically novel, coming through. We stand at The Edge before the Ocean (another Living Symbol): The Ocean of Vision.

The Edge is that place where we stand open to Being. Our standing, however, must be a standing from somewhere—once again, we speak here of a concrete life situation, but a situation within the context of our larger, contemporary, Postmodern world. The Edge is that place where the everyday world breaks off and that which is beyond world can open to us as a coming-to-us. The Edge is this Opening to Being...the Opening-to-us of Being. That-which-opens-to-us—if we look out over the abyss of an Ocean—has the horizon of futurity—it has a future orientation...we are artist / poet visionaries, perhaps even prophets.

Mythos would no longer be only otherworldly focused (which was the case for most traditional religions, especially in the Piscean Age) but grounded in our connectedness to Earth. It would emerge organically out of a place since it must begin somewhere.

> *The Mythos begins somewhere*
> *and must begin with someone.*

So we can literally also live in places of The Edge—physically, geographically... places that evoke in us the sense of an edge, where a break occurs, of vistas, of endings and beginnings, places that open us to some other reality. Coastlines are especially powerful here...and mountainous regions, canyons, terrains that abruptly shift...even in the midst of a desert all around us, the quiet, extreme solitude, the loneliness, the stark desolation that rips us out of familiar Human Reality... Here in America, the whole long West Coast especially, Big Sur famously; there are the Rocky Mountains, Sierra Nevada, Cascades, Mt. Shasta especially...the Mojave Desert, Monument Valley, Grand Canyon, across New Mexico, Arizona...the Nevada expanses devoid of any signs of civilization... We could obviously name hundreds of other geographical places around the planet. And perhaps others will.

These are places of The Edge…places where the veils of human Illusion are thin, tenuous; places revealing the translucent glow of something other… of uncanny Spirit coming through…

In places of The Edge, we become sensitive to living at the boundary between worlds. There is always the familiar, established, collective world behind us… and there is the invitation, the summons, to open up to something other beyond. Of course, most do not experience this at all. Oh, perhaps they get a fleeting glimpse of it, and then it's gone. They undoubtedly must realize, though, these are so often places of beauty. These places of The Edge at the fringes of civilization, outside of mainstream culture, are so often simply considered vacation spots, places to drive through, yes, places of momentary experiences of beauty…and what's next?

But even cities can be located at The Edge. Here, on the West Coast, I can think of no better big cities than San Francisco and Los Angeles, cities at The Edge of our American continent, cities that are at The Edge of It All—they are Postmodern par excellence, and yet sitting at The Edge of the Ocean of possible new Vision.

Here I live, and think, in Santa Cruz (county), on Monterey Bay, also at The Edge of our American continent. Years ago, living within the city, I would stand on the cliffs (West Cliff Dr.) that fall to the Pacific…the vast All-One-Ocean-of-oceans… Here, on the California West Coast, this is where our Postmodern civilization has reached its peak, come to its full expression— think of Silicon Valley, just over the Santa Cruz Mountains—but this is also where it all comes to an end, this is The Edge beyond which is the Ocean of Vision, of New Age Vision…

Places, we must realize, have sleeping within them their own Mythos significance, which is to say, they have the potential of Mythos. Let us be clear about it, to speak of The Edge, we are speaking Mythos. Because it is Mythos, the professors will probably not be discussing this in their classes. This requires that first we come to attune ourselves to our being in a place, and by doing so, we become aware of the powers at play in this place, and what its character is; we articulate then such powers into Form—we bring into Form the Mythos of place. We must bring forth then a place into its story (its Mythos) within the greater global Story (the developing Mythos of the Age). We cannot accept Postmodernist thought that would deny us an existential significance to place, that we might have in fact a Story to tell, that there might indeed be a great, New Story to tell. Postmodernist thought, we should keep in mind, is anti-narrative, against Story. Opening ourselves, attuning ourselves, articulating the Mythos of place, we can no longer consider ourselves in this regard Postmodern.

How Mythos of place ties into the greater Mythos of the Age is an even greater challenge. I call that greater Mythos today *The Mythos*, indicating that it must be global, universal, not limited to any one Tradition or ethnic cultural myth from the past. I will be sharing much more about *The Mythos* over time...

To be a poet of place means that you have tapped into the latent Mythos of your place. Latent means that a Mythos has not yet been fully articulated, has not yet fully come into Form. That would be the work of the poet—to bring that Mythos into Language, to write of it and to be able to speak of it. And yes, I have written of, and lectured on, Santa Cruz, its Mythos of place.

When I speak of The Edge, experienced as place, I am speaking from the West Coast, at The Edge of the Western continent. Here, in Santa Cruz, on Monterey Bay, on the West Coast, in California, I stand on The Edge of the continent. I found my way here many, many years ago and came to realize that here I stood, at The Edge. Our Postmodern sensibility has forgotten the power that place has. We should realize how a place can be articulated into Mythos, and for us personally, it can be the locus of Mythos significance in our life. A place can be where a rebirth, a transformation, has happened, where a life-changing Vision was received. But Mythos, of course, goes transpersonal—we are in fact tapping into a larger narrative than our own personal story.

But why do I insist on place, with regard to such a notion as The Edge? Because The Edge is not simply an abstract concept, but as a Living Symbol, integral with Mythos, it is psychospiritually concrete. And by concrete, we

29

mean that places have their own power, places can be psychospiritual portals, places can be sacred. Any potential new religion, for example, of Gaia, will be grounded in our relationship to place. (We also hear of the term "regional.")

Once we are attuned in such a way that we can stand at The Edge, we are then ready for a more radical Edge…

So, then, where is this place that is the more radical Edge? If we stand here on the West Coast of America—as I stand here on the coast of California—, do we only say, The Edge of America? Shall we not say, The Edge of Western Civilization? Shall we not say, The Edge of our Postmodern world? Shall we not say, But this indeed is The Edge of our entire global civilization? And shall we not say, The Edge of our possible entire biosphere collapse, as the climate scientists are warning us of? And shall we then say, The Edge of possible civilization collapse? And then, shall we say, The Edge where we can see before us an MELE (mass extinction level event) already underway? But… but…shall we also be so bold as to say, perhaps as delusional visionaries to say, that this is The Edge of a new evolutionary dispensation, what we shall be calling the "New Age"? That before us is the Ocean of Vision?

* * *

Perhaps I have been pulling a surprise all along by mentioning the New Age. Didn't the New Age come and go back in the late 20th Century? Didn't it all come down to a cultural fad…the New Age "movement"? But more critically, how can we even speak about a New Age, when we are suggesting at the same time the very real possibility of near-term human extinction (NTHE)? Whatever one might have believed about the New Age, that is, the New Age was a faddish, airy-fairy, feel-good cultural movement that is now passé, there will nonetheless come some New Age upon Earth. As astrologers, we speak of the new Aquarian Age.

Why do I bring in the New Age here? Because we live in a time of the transition between astrological Ages. I have explored all of this in detail in my book *The New Age Vision*, so I see no need to restate everything I said there. The question is, Are we not transitioning into a whole new world orientation before our eyes? The sooner we see that, the sooner we can truly stand at The Edge and be open to new Vision, to novelty on a scale that is simply overwhelming. Even if civilization is nearing The Edge of possible collapse, that does not negate the metaphysical reality that another Age, another chapter, of the human Story is simultaneously beginning.

We can easily use a stronger word here, and that is transformation. We live in a time not only of profound transition, but an Age that calls for our radical transforming of this Postmodern world. We are called to be transformers... let us be so bold:

The Transformer

Who gazes into night & a new Intelligence in the stars
      can see?
Who stands open to inspiration to receive what launches
      peoples into futurity?
Who absorbs age-old Tradition, the ancient arts of wisdom,
      Earthwide the panoply of cultures,
but says, I am not a puppet of the past,
I am not a hand-me-down child of other peoples
      & cultures—
I recognize all, absorb all, but what I absorb I transform.

Who says, I do not accept what lies dead at my feet—
Let the old God be dead, for new Divinity will live
      through me!
Let the dead return to the soil & enrich the soil—
Who says, I love enrichment of the soil.

Whose feet are planted firmly upon the body of Earth,
who absorbs Minerals, Air & Water, Fire of Sun,
whose essence of Self is seed of the new Tree?
Who says, I attune myself to a new Spirit coming among us,
I attune myself to the superconscious energies of Neptune,
      Pluto & Uranus,

I attune myself to the Milky Way galactic influx of new
    Intelligence.
Who says, Through me the new Vision of Ages manifests
    its evolutionary intention—
All I absorb is made new through me.

Who says, I am a Transformer!
I transform my conditioning, my complexes, my fears,
    my insecurities, into strengths & psychospiritual tools
    of Psyche.
I transform the woe-is-me, whining voice of my sufferings
    into the Story of my struggles.
I transform decadent & dying culture into new riches
    to be shared.
I transform old obscured ways into a new path shining
    in the Labyrinth.
I transform the barrage of daily impression into insight,
    unconnected information into knowledge, stale doctrine
    into living wisdom.
I transform the art I work in, the childhood religion
    I outgrew.
I transform the self I was.

Who says, I am a Transformer!
I transform the past into a Vision of futurity!
Who says, I extend my hand to others & freely offer them
    the fruits of futurity!

* * *

The New Age has been referred to and can be referred to in various other locutions: the new consciousness, the new spirituality, the new paradigm, the Awakening, the Quickening, the Shift, the Great Shift of the Ages, the dawning Age of Aquarius, the Event Horizon, the Event of Appropriation (from Heidegger), and today, currently, it's *The Great Awakening*. All are ways of dancing around the phrase "New Age." Indeed, the same could be said for

"Postmodern." There are those who want to believe that the Postmodern Era had passed years ago, so they cleverly think to use the phrase Post-Postmodern. Or there is a supposed current, new movement, the Metamodern. And yet, to me, they are but variations on Postmodern, the era that still defines this transition between Ages that we are living in.

Is this current stirring (is it a movement?) among many of an Awakening—a Great Awakening—happening today really "new"? Are so many but starting over what the New Age movement had already initiated back in the latter 20th Century? Whatever its supposed shortcomings at that time, the New Age movement was only beginning to break out into the culture and had already initiated this Awakening. We must be aware of the mainstream dominated by a power elite agenda to highjack, co-opt, manipulate movements to disempower them, always keeping the populace jumping to the next Big Thing. Okay, the New Age movement acquired some cultural traction, but it was time to sidetrack it. So now it's the Great Awakening as if it is something new. We must beware of what the agenda of the power elite will come up with next...will the Great Awakening be co-opted too, sooner or later? And we could just as readily bring up the Sixties Spirit—what happened to it? (The Sixties Spirit in many ways did merge into the New Age movement.)

The New Age breaks from Postmodernism in regard to two fundamental themes: 1) Being: a reaffirmation of our relationship to Being, our new encounter with Being, and 2) creativity: affirming our right to a profound existential creativity, implying a revived metaphysical, spiritual creativity, which we will refer to as *Mythos*. Both of these refer to the discovery of The Fountain of Unlimited Creativity.

I find that most who somewhat understand that we live in a transition between Ages still don't take it seriously enough. I am referring especially, ironically, to the metaphysical/spiritual communities. The assumption has been that we can still carry over Traditions as they have been passed down to us, as is. As if creative transformation of our Traditions isn't necessary. As if the radical novelty of Spirit coming-to-us anew doesn't enter the picture. A New Age is a most profound shift, challenging us to the utmost of our existence. So few even understand this challenge!

Those of us who speak for the New Age, if we are to think what today we are being called to think, if we are to be thinkers of the New Age, we must begin thinking then from The Edge. There are of course many questions packed into that statement, and I hope to unpack here much of all that that implies.

* * *

Is it true that we, collectively, are standing at The Edge already? Here, we are talking about all of us, without exception, all seven plus billion of us currently living on planet Earth. Only a few, though, have come to fully realize this current reality of The Edge. We who speak from the Postmodern Edge of our civilization, a one world civilization that embraces the entire Earth, find ourselves standing at an Edge beyond which is an abyss—it is the possible ending of everything, literally everything, that we have ever known and loved. Let us be blunt about it—this abyss beyond The Edge is the very real possibility of the collapse and end of our civilization. How long can one stand here, in dread, gazing into such darkness and horror of what may come, and not want to immediately step back from it, even run back, to more familiar ground—perhaps to another Story? Ah, to step back to a more optimistic Story! and to the familiar comforts of life that we might know. Ah, to step back and forget the Vision we have seen. How long can one stare into such an abyss and not think this is all but a nightmare that we will awaken from? That this is only a dystopian science fiction movie that we can all walk out of the theatre from? But no, if we have been awake, The Edge is all too real. Instead of turning our eyes away, we will look into that abyss, and we will think seriously, courageously, even as we slightly tremble as we stand at The Edge…The Edge of such a precipice. Might there be anything resembling an answer out there, in the beyond, if we choose to stand here, at The Edge, long enough? If we can withstand gazing, in other words, into catastrophe…into human finitude…into nothingness?

There are those who will want to argue that The Edge that I speak of doesn't exist, that it is a hoax—as for example, that global warming / climate change is a hoax, an alarmist exaggeration, perhaps a well-meaning but misplaced concern, that it is not as bad as all that; at best, it is premature to speak about such an Edge as the collapse of our global civilization…of human extinction. The well-respected British biologist David Attenborough, however—and many others we could name…James Lovelock, James Hanson, Guy McPherson…—doesn't think this is premature at all.

How can one be a thinker at The Edge without bringing up the contemporary climate issue…climate change? Thinkers in the past simply took the Earth and the relatively stable climate of the geophysical Holocene Era for granted. Earth and Her climate were a consistent background that thinkers didn't even have to address, didn't even have to refer to, in their philosophical works, even up to the Postmodernists. But we are now living, according to a number of geophysical scientists (and this is still a controversial issue) in the geophysical Anthropocene Era, having begun roughly back in the mid-20th Century, which, curiously enough, coincided with the beginnings of the Postmodern cultural age.

Increasingly we hear people asking, How much time do we have left? Realize that this is not a religious question about End Times, but is rather an empirical, scientific question that is based on CO2 and methane levels, the melting of the Arctic icecap and the melting of Antarctica, of glaciers melting in Greenland and on all the major mountain ranges, the acidification of the oceans, the increasing warming of the oceans, inducing radically changing ocean currents, the increase in extreme heat waves that are already killing thousands, etc. As Finnish president Sauli Niinistö has said, *If we lose the Arctic, we lose civilization.* The fact that more people are awakening to this relatively near-term possibility marks a radical shift in our view of civilization. Other civilizations of the past have fallen, but then other civilizations in the same timeframe still flourished. The thing is, we are talking here of an entire global civilization. That we are this vulnerable regarding our collective finitude, how many have even taken this seriously yet?

Is our mainstream culture preparing at all for any of this? But shouldn't the first question be, Is our mainstream culture even talking about this? Yes, the possible scenarios about global warming, for example, are making more news—we constantly hear more about climate change—but the seriousness of it is still held at bay. The public must not panic about this; the Status Quo must be maintained at all cost. There is still time to imagine that we will get through this. There is still time, the mainstream says, usually meaning, we still have until the end of this century before the situation becomes dire.

What complicates the climate change issue is the controversial topic of geoengineering. Some type of geoengineering program has been proposed as a solution to global warming. But is there in fact an active geoengineering program (one version is solar radiation management (SRM)) or not? We look up in our skies and often see what are called chemtrails: jet airliners at relatively low altitudes spewing out parallel lines and grids that linger for periods of time that blur and whiten out blue skies. The "official" mainstream scientific word about this is that they are only contrails; or they neglect to address the issue altogether. But there are questions here that for me go unanswered. I am not about to get into all the details concerning chemtrails or contrails here but have only hinted at the general controversial issue.

Let us briefly lay out the various debatable positions on this complex issue of climate change:

There are those who say that the climate isn't significantly changing at all (ignoring what nearly 100% of climate scientists are saying). What we see today are just climate variations that have always occurred in the past.

There are those who say climate change is a hoax perpetrated by mainstream officialdom (no mention of geoengineering) for some ulterior motive.

There are those who say climate change is a hoax and that geoengineering isn't happening, it's mere conspiracy theory.

There are those who say climate change is real and geoengineering is mere conspiracy theory, not happening.

There are those who say climate change is a hoax but there is a geoengineering program underway that is screwing with our weather… it is already an ongoing weather modification program.

There are those who say geoengineering is the sole culprit for major changes in our climate, but it's a covert program with possible ulterior motives. But why can't people see it for themselves.

There are those who say climate change is caused by human activity (a CO2 level rise caused by the use of fossil fuels) and forget about any geoengineering conspiracy.

There are those who say any climate changes that are actually real are not human caused but are caused by natural solar cycles. Climate scientists have studied this and say that any solar influence on current climate change is negligible.

There are those who say the climate has always changed through the eons and humans have nothing to do with it. We just have to live with it.

There are those who say a covert geoengineering program is already underway in an attempt to address our increasingly serious climate issue, and why can't people look up and see it for themselves.

There are those who say that thousands are misguided by what they believe they see as chemtrails (geoengineering)...what they see are only contrails. This is whether climate is an issue or not.

There are those who say both are implicated in climate change—human-caused activity and a geoengineering program that appears to have gone rogue...making climate change worse or having negative impacts on natural regions.

There are those who say the Earth is actually cooling, whether geoengineering is involved or not, or is ever mentioned. This is contrary to what 100% of climate scientists say, and even what those of us who have followed rising global temperatures over the years have noticed.

Now climate change is a complex issue involving controversial views, but, yes, I am aware of those who prefer to simplify it, who will immediately say, for example, it's all a hoax, there is no need to further discuss it. They might add, though, Earth has always had climate cycles, so what? Yes, but these—we are talking major—climate cycles can last for hundreds, if not thousands, of years. We, today, happen to be living in the Here and Now. Are we preparing for extreme climate changes—of course also known as global warming—that might collapse our civilization, as increasingly more are warning of? Do we have an obligation to future generations? I find that most people are not really concerned. They say, Let the power elite and the scientific community worry about it.

Now if we take climate change seriously, the obvious question that comes up is, What is causing it? The common, mainstream scientific view is that it is human caused. That now becomes a controversial issue. In what way is humanity behind it? Primarily the use of fossil fuels. But now we bring geoengineering—aka chemtrails in our skies—into the picture. Geoengineering allegedly is advocated, sooner or later, to help reduce global warming. But then, are the "chemtrails" we see actually making the atmosphere more erratic? The worry over the increase in human caused $CO2$ in the atmosphere is just a hoax, some say, promoted by the Great Reset elite. The "chemtrails" are what is aggravating our atmosphere. Of course, there are those who say that currently active geoengineering is mere conspiracy theory...it isn't happening. The thing is, though, geoengineering is actually a currently valid scientific field of research. But if...if indeed it is currently ongoing, the question is then, why is the geoengineering program covert to begin with? Has it been helping, but the (secret) government prefers not to make it public? Why? Not to alarm the public? Might it be that human $CO2$ caused climate change should not upset the corporate Status Quo? I am aware that most people want simple answers Yes or No regarding this complex issue. I remain open to questions but do largely follow climate researcher Dane Wigington on all of this since he is passionate about it and is conversant with all sides of the issue. Elana Freeland has also written three quite dense, well documented, researched books on the subject of geoengineering.

We should keep in mind an Air Force document that came out back in the late Nineties titled, "Weather as a Force Multiplier: We Own the Weather in 2025." And yes, 2025 is now already here. Is it possible that the Air Force could put into effect a weather modification program without years of preceding prototype efforts…without an active geoengineering program leading up to 2025?

Those who don't take the geoengineering of our skies seriously—it's all mere conspiracy theory—should pause a moment and ask a few questions. First, as I've said, we know that geoengineering is a bona fide scientific field already allegedly for the (future) purpose of alleviating global warming. Right? It is not being funded as some secret science fiction joke. It is also called Solar Radiation Management (SRM). So, when would the geoengineering program be employed? When global temperatures get much hotter? Let's wait until the Arctic icecap melts? When there are food shortages? Let's wait until the biosphere shows serious signs of collapse? So you think that geoengineering would be employed in time? One response to this question of when might be, geoengineering, in the sense of aerial spraying, wouldn't be employed until it was considered safe. Oh, really? How incredibly naïve that sounds. Can the chemical spraying of our skies ever be considered safe? And who decides that? Now, would an active geoengineering program ever be announced to the public? Or would it be clandestine, so as not to create any fearful concern that civilization might indeed be in jeopardy? Last, what would the chemical spraying of our skies look like? Wouldn't it look pretty much identical to today's so-called "chemtrails"? Would it look like excessive chemtrails? Would it be then much more pronounced? More obvious? Would the spraying be laid out in parallel lines and grids as the so-called "chemtrails" are? Even if kept secret, would it still be obvious enough that the public would definitely begin to wonder, What the heck is going on? Or would the geoengineers choose instead some other modality? Some researchers will claim that satellite systems and HAARP have already been involved in the covert geoengineering program, that aerosol spraying ("chemtrails") is only one aspect of it.

So we listen to the doomers' gospel of abrupt climate change and the collapse of civilization and of our coming human extinction. I do take what they are telling us seriously; I have given them a bit of coverage in my writings. They have pulled together the scientific facts, the alarming graphs, the research of hundreds of climate scientists. We thank them for this powerful dose of awareness. Guy McPherson, for one, is certainly intent on putting this in our face. Yet, what I find dissatisfying about the alarmists is their narrow, single Vision. The primary spokespersons are all generally scientific types, for one. After they offer us their assessment of what the trends are showing, what advice, then, do they give us, as to how to respond to this? That is, what advice about confronting this? The last thing we hear, what they would want to offer is hope. They have a word for this—*hopium*. By and large, their suggestions are platitudes. They will say, Enjoy your life, while there is still time. Appreciate Nature, while you can. Do what you love to do. Love is everything. So, is this the best they can offer? These scientists, these professors, who have enjoyed their status academic careers, their good life as respectable professionals, are going to advise us on existential, spiritual matters? They come across as conventional, mainstream-conditioned intellectuals. They are not big thinkers at all. Excuse me, professor, thank you for the facts regarding our possible extinction, but I don't need to be lectured about the basic existential lessons of life. Do what I love to do? You like to write poetry, you say to me—well, write poetry then. Excuse me, I am a visionary poet—is that okay? Can you understand that? Or is that not conventional enough? Does that not fit into your properly educated view of mere poetry? My being a visionary, meaning, my having a Vision, goes far beyond your scientific studied Vision of doom. My visionary work might appear to be…what, another case of hopium, delusional? But, still, *Do what you love to do.*

I have not heard any doomers expressing an understanding of Mythos, though their doom scenario could be a preliminary Form of Mythos. They say nothing about the larger picture, that we are living in a transition period between Ages. They say nothing about a new spiritual dispensation coming through. They have nothing to say about Reality beyond our Human Reality. There seems to be no interest in the divine dimension of human being. No understanding of the psychospiritual. No hint at all that Other Intelligences are watching Earth and are well aware of what is unfolding on Earth. They have no sense that Others have an agenda with Earth, and no sense that such an agenda might involve the New Age. Civilizations have come and gone, and there have always been Ages upon Earth.

Former professor of conservation biology Guy McPherson has dedicated his life now to bringing us the bad news. Yes, he is an extremist doomer, which should not make us disinclined, however, to actually listen to what he has to say. But his near-term projected timeframe back in about 2014 for the collapse of civilization has been seriously premature. He was saying back then that by 2025 civilization would be collapsing and by about 2030 most of humanity would be extinct. His alarmist voice, however, is rarely heard these days, probably because of his extremist view.

Imagine what might be coming. The droughts, the desertification of huge swaths of land, so that no crops can grow, no water is to be found, that will force the migration of millions of people. To where? Intolerable heat waves that kill thousands. Widespread, absolutely destructive wildfires, such as many countries are already experiencing. Imagine the super-storms wreaking unprecedented havoc, no longer on a once in a century basis, but yearly. Now we imagine the suffering of untold millions and billions of people driven to homelessness…starvation…the conflict over resources… When infrastructure breaks down, the chaos in mega-cities of multimillions… The great militaries taking things into their own hands after civil law fails.

Is it surprising that I have given Mythos Form to Nihil [*The Book of Nihil in The Mythos*], the God of nihilism?

Lest we are too human centered here, too human Ego incestuous, let us mull over what is happening to the biosphere, let us show some feelings about the untold millions of creatures that are perishing. It is said that already up to 60% of all wildlife on the planet is gone. We already notice for ourselves the fewer animals, fewer birds, reptiles, especially amphibians… Nature is slowly going silent. The biologists tell us that we are currently in the 6th great mass extinction. It is said that the great oceans are dying. Every other week now we hear of mass die-offs on the West Coast—of sea stars, of fish, of sea lions, seals, of seabirds…thousands, even tens of thousands, of seabirds at one time. Whales washing up on shores. Orcas no longer giving birth. Of course, one could argue that any one of these developments is part of cyclic Nature; they could be reversed with appropriate efforts. Yes? No? We might also bring into the picture radiation going into the Pacific Ocean from Fukushima, Japan, the major nuclear reactor disaster that occurred on March 11, 2011, after a great 9.0 earthquake took place out in the Pacific Ocean off the Japanese coast causing a tremendous tsunami to sweep into the Fukashima Daiichi nuclear power plant. An explosion took place in one of the three reactors spreading plutonium and various other radionuclides into the atmosphere, into countrysides—perhaps all the way to Tokyo—, and into the ocean. It is projected that the radiation will remain active for centuries. And now Japan is dumping tons of radioactive water that it can no longer keep on site, into the Pacific. And the three reactors are still dangerously molten…

We are alarmed to hear this news. We are saddened by the loss of the creatures we share this once life-rich, super-abundant, glorious Earth with. One day we may not hear the birds sing. One day we may not see the thousands of waterfowl on the lakes and marshes. One day we may not see any seabirds on the shores of the ocean. Tide pools empty. The fish gone. One day the oceans might be one lifeless, acidified, chemical soup…the so-called Canfield Ocean event.

A profound shift in psyche will undoubtedly take place among the surviving remnant of any MELE [mass extinction level event], if there indeed comes the ominous future of an MELE…and if there is a human remnant still alive. This remnant will be the new Aquarians, as they would now be living in the Aquarian Age.

The Revelation of humanity's possible finitude—this is a Revelation that we would rather not bring up. But bring it up as the first of possible Revelations I did. There is uncomfortably another possibility of humanity's finitude to bring up—that will be next. But, then, other possible evolutionary Revelations we will explore…

* * *

It has been concerning to me that I keep seeing Earth spelled out in print with a small 'e.' What an insult, a travesty, that writers would not give our Earth the dignity of a proper name: capital E: Earth. The other planets are always printed with capitals: Mercury, Venus, Mars, Jupiter, Saturn, etc. We see this lapse in respect in print across the board: in Nature books, ecology books, environmental publications, ecological writers who should know better, mainstream blurbs, channeled books, spiritual books, in journalism and commentary. Even in books by otherwise highly conscious, Nature-sensitive authors, we find this appalling oversight. We demote Earth to a lower-case status that makes it easier for a capitalist world to exploit. To go so far as to refer to Earth as the living Gaia is far too much for the mainstream. But starting with Earth as a proper name is the least we can do:

My Dear Earth

My Dear Earth—
Why can they not get it right?
Why can they not print your name properly?
All too often I find you slighted; I cringe
when they give you this small, common, merely thing name.
You, the living glory of our home, you are entitled to be
    the proper name of our planet.
Other planets are so honored, you deserve likewise—
One might think it were some kind of conspiracy.
Earth, can they not show respect, learn the printing
of your name properly, boldly, beginning with a capital E.

My dear Earth, this is my hope—
That all from now on will be able to read
your correct name, your proper name:

      Capital E – a – r – t – h

* * *

Another example of The Edge that we face every minute of every day, every week, every month, every year, is the constant threat of nuclear annihilation. As long as nations possess nuclear weapons, humanity is not safe from itself. Nuclear weapons are a madness, an insanity of global perverse Reason. We have heard since our childhood we need nuclear weapons to deter other nations from threatening us and using them against us. This is rationality become so twisted that it is no wonder that we live in a Postmodern nihilistic world.

Nuclear weapons show a fundamental, utter disregard for humanity. They are the supreme example of Human Unevolved Darkness, a phrase that I have begun using and developing.

As I've noted earlier, the marker year in my thinking that inaugurated the Postmodern Era was 1945, specifically July and August of 1945, when the Bomb was first tested and when the Bomb was then used on two Japanese cities.

That nuclear physicists work for the military nuclear weapons program is downright shameful, and I mean this globally. Even Oppenheimer, director of the Manhattan Project to make the original Bomb, and other scientists involved, radically changed their minds about the Bomb after it was used on Japan, with the realization that the further deployment of the Bomb would only bring humanity to a most dangerous Edge. Oppenheimer was against the making of the hydrogen bomb. Einstein, who signed a letter to President Rosevelt (actually written by Leo Szilard) encouraging the making of this potentially tremendous new weapon, the atomic bomb, before the Germans could make it, regretted it for the rest of his life. But when the Bomb was first tested and detonated and a number of the scientists witnessed how awesomely powerful it was, they quickly were foolishly thinking at first that it must and would bring about peace in the world. It was as if it were a Revelation to them that would inaugurate peace among the nations. How incredibly naïve and deluded they were. It was rather a Revelation that eventually was called MAD…Mutual Assured Destruction.

The fact that global nuclear weapon arsenals could destroy our civilization in even one day, on almost a moment's, even unexpected, notice, and that the nations are not passionately doing anything about eliminating this hellish nightmare we continue to live in, is unconscionable, literally pathological. The majority of global leaders, military leaders, of the nuclear nations, we will have to say, are psychopathic. Of course they function well enough in their leadership roles in a sick society. We continue to live on possible borrowed time. Global societies have for decades been conditioned not to think about it, not to dwell upon it. I, for one, think about it all the time. Until nuclear weapons are eliminated, I will continue to call this current Postmodern civilization pathological. Nations have gone MAD. Of course, I have not been the only one to say this...

The MADness that is Nuclear Weapons

They make no sense. No rational sense at all.
Unless rational—Logos—has a MADness hiding within it,
      a death wish—
Did Freud not suggest Thanatos was hiding within us?
What pathological sense do weapons of mass destruction,
oh, but let us be blunt about it—weapons built for human
      annihilation, make?
The nuclear scientists who started us on this path
that could only lead to Hell, would ideally have been
brought forward before some council & held accountable.
To name them all? unfortunately including Einstein—
He regretted his signing a letter to President Roosevelt
advocating for the Bomb to the end of his life.

Let us be more blunt about this—
Nuclear weapons are an abomination, my citizens
      of the world,
an evil that world culture in the 20th Century found
      acceptable.
Rationalized as a necessity of National Security, a necessity
that was cynically called Mutual Assured Destruction...
      aka MAD, in other words, MADness.
Let us call out these wayward nations:
The United States, Russia, China, England,
France, India, Pakistan, North Korea—
Does Israel have such weapons? They say probably yes—
are sick at the core of their collective psyche.
How else can we put it? That they are ignorant

of the Nihil within their own psyche,
so they might be excused for such ignorance?

These nations would kill, eliminate, millions upon millions,
    possibly billions,
and radiation suffering imposed upon millions more,
the death of untold billions of creatures,
glorious cities leveled, centuries of human culture
utterly devastated, reduced to nothing,
a nuclear winter death spread across the globe…

Do not make pathetic excuses, do not turn a blind eye,
enough of your petty tit-for-tat negotiations
that have done nothing to stop this MADness—
There is absolutely no sane reason for conscious beings
to maintain weapons of nuclear mass death—
I am addressing you—leaders of nations, politicians,
military men, scientists, who all traffic in death, death, death.

Let the horrifying icon of the Mushroom Cloud be gone,
    be gone!

December 20, 2019

* * *

Oh, but lest we forget the Cold War. Indeed, the specter of the Mushroom Cloud signaled the Postmodern Era (mid-Twentieth Century), in which civilization experienced its collective disorientation before the Cosmos. Political and corporate mainstream culture certainly kept the public numbingly forgetful of this. The thought that seems unbelievable (annihilation) has been hidden in Human Unevolved Darkness for decades. Thanatos, the Death Wish, hiding in that Darkness, as Freud spoke of a century ago.

When we speak about the possibilities of Revelation today, this is another one we'd rather not bring up—the very real possibility of humanity's finitude. Thinking from The Edge, I have had to bring human finitude up first, though

I would have rather it would be the last mention of possible Revelations in our future. For other Revelations are possible...

* * *

War is insanity. Let me repeat that again: War is utter insanity. Violence, killing, inflicting suffering upon peoples, terrorism, invading other countries, military arsenals whose aim is killing and destruction, engaging in war, any of this and all of this is anymore the insanity of our Human Unevolved Darkness. The New Age dispensation of Higher Self does not accept excuses for any of this in Human Reality. Which implies that our spiritual Light must be engaged in this unevolved Darkness and bring to Light, into the open, what insanity thrives in this Darkness. Some will wish to call it evil. Well, yes, so then what? Whether individuals, gangs, factions, power-hungry leaders, whole countries, a secret power elite, a global elite conspiring for world control, at any level of intent to do violence, to bring suffering upon others, their intentions must be exposed, their insanity must be brought into some Form of public therapy. Yes, that is unheard of, but in the New Age all is to be brought out into the open Air. Another challenge for Mythos.

When we consider global conflicts and wars, past and present, we find that rulers, leaders, despots, governments, a power elite, terrorist groups, what have you, will simply assume, We have a right to kill people. The question is, What gives them that right? Do they have reasons for killing others? What they would assume would be valid reasons? From the perspective of an enlightened psyche, though, we can consider them psychopathic. From the perspective of an enlightened psyche, there are no valid reasons for killing others. There are no valid excuses. Killing others is psychopathic, period. They all succumb to Human Unevolved Darkness. In the New Age I envision as a visionary, this will no longer be excusable.

I hear some saying that today the world is actually devolving before our eyes, that it's in fact all over for us. What are we to respond to this? This is not at all the New Age dispensation. Yes, the transition between Ages can be filled with various crises, cultural confusion, a cosmic disorientation. But there are many of us today who represent a new Spirit coming into the world, a Great Awakening, a Revelation of new Divinity to transform this decadent, nihilistic, Postmodern transition period between Ages we are currently living in. We are those who tell of a New Story of humanity's evolutionary trajectory.

* * *

There is no denying it—the Mythos of The Edge is real and needs to be brought into its Form.

Very few are fully aware of The Edge. Even among artists, poets, writers, I note there is little explicit mention of The Edge, or any other key symbol that would be its equivalent. Be that as it may at this time, that will inevitably change. This is my prophecy: As our civilization approaches The Edge, as it becomes ever more apparent that we are indeed at The Edge, we are going to see the emergence of more visionaries. All manner of visionaries and prophets. Increasingly artists and poets will tire of the revolving door of Postmodern decadence; they will come to see how much of a dead end the Postmodern has become. The visionary door will blast wide open. This is to be expected. When crisis looms over us comes opportunity—the breakthrough to new Vision. The realization occurs that a new existential orientation in our lives is demanded. A desperate people will produce individuals desperate to share new Vision.

To be a visionary today, that is, a philosopher-poet-spiritual visionary, writing and sharing about the Advent of new Divinity coming-into the world, is certainly controversial, to say the least. You are going to be open to criticism, attack, discredit, utter misunderstanding, from others, especially coming from Fundamentalists and staunch Traditionalists of the various religions. It is undoubtedly assumed by some that visionaries of my kind are anachronistic, no longer necessary, and even not wanted. The more public you become, the more your work gets better known, the criticism, the attacks, will predictably increase.

New Divinity? Yes, we are referring to a radical new Revelation that new Divinity is coming-into Human Reality. Traditional Jews, Christians, and

Muslims will have a definite difficulty in even accepting the possibility of the Advent of new Divinity in our world. Would they even be open to hearing of such a possibility? And that a poet is the one who is announcing the Advent of this new Divinity of Psyche? Who could take a poet making such a grandiose claim seriously? He must be crazy. And easily dismissed. And if he is heard, he would certainly have to be prepared for getting attacked from various quarters for making such a claim.

A key question, What would it take for such a new Revelation to find acceptance in the culture? Would people just take the word of a poet regarding his visionary experience at face value? Must others receive their own Visions confirming such a Revelation? Must there first come some radical revolution in consciousness? Must the poet begin to gather followers? Must miracles come into the picture? Must this poet or someone with the same/similar Vision be performing miracles? Would this new Divinity have to appear to others in miraculous, paranormal ways? Must there appear signs and wonders in the heavens? Of course, some would immediately think that Other Intelligence is involved, that is, ETs. Then must ETs put in an undeniable public appearance? Must there first occur some global catastrophe? Must civilization be about to collapse before a new Revelation is heralded?

Of course in our Postmodern context, any question regarding a new Revelation announced by a poet, or anyone, finding acceptance in the culture could be simply answered: Our Postmodern world is pluralistic—anyone can promote any wild, crazy, outrageous, radical idea, claim, belief, Vision, and the culture just accommodates it—and just as readily disempowers it—among countless other voices clamoring out there. Our Postmodern context is a cultural smorgasbord of just about anything you can think of...

To claim that we are thinking from The Edge of the world: One might ask, Is that possible? Doesn't Human Reality totally condition us, totally interpret everything for us? Are we not thrown into the matrix of the always already of Human Reality interpretation? First, we must realize that the always already is not fixed but is itself always undergoing change, always shifting, always opening new avenues of thought. Did Derrida and Deleuze actually teach us something or not?

To stand at The Edge is to stand where the totality of human interpreted reality breaks off. What we call our world—worldhood, as Heidegger would call it—is this totality of ready-made interpretations, going into the fabric of Language itself, so that everything appears immediately understandable in some fashion. For example, we find this with the phrase 'New Age' itself: It appears that everyone already understands what is meant by it and therefore can dismiss it or file it away as some fad born of previous decades, which is how the mainstream would prefer to see it. And yet, very few genuinely understand it. The New Age is a spiritual frontier…appearing at The Edge… at the Event Horizon.

There is the more intellectually popular current notion regarding new "myth," and that is, that fantasy fiction, science fiction, and the like, especially as delivered in movies, is assumed to satisfy our need for "myth" today. Oh, really? Make myth safe, entertaining, completely commodified, framed within a capitalist agenda. Yes, satisfy your deeper psyche by going to see a movie. To assume that a visionary poet would satisfy his Vision by going to sci fi movies is absurd. Well, it certainly does not satisfy our need—or, should I say, my need—for Mythos. Which is one hint why I keep focused on "Mythos" rather than the co-opted cultural coin of "myth."

* * *

Mythos, understood in the most universal way, is our being open to having a direct relationship with Being—and this implies how Being is showing itself to us via Spirit in the Appropriation of Being with Human Reality in this current time and bringing this relationship—which is a creative process, a co-creative process par excellence—into Form, which implies then the telling of a New Story. (I have taken the "Appropriation of Being" from Heidegger and have now made it integral to my own thinking. Succinctly put, it implies that Being, short of us having a purely mystical experience of Being, is never revealed to us in some absolute totality but only that which Being has appropriated to Human Reality via Time (history), which is called the Zeitgeist (Time Spirit), what I also refer to as the World Fabric. And lest there be any misunderstanding here, we must not confuse Being with any human-like motive, intention, decision, with anything human, whatsoever. Perhaps thousands of Other Intelligences in the universe have a relationship to Being. And in the same vein, Being is not a "God" who "watches" over us. To speak about Being per se is to venture into mystical experience.) To continue: So there is no dependency on famous movie directors feeding us commodified, entertainment doses of action-packed "myth." It is we ourselves who are called to actively bring forth Mythos from out of our own existential situation, our own gnosis, into the culture. It is we who have had this firsthand encounter with Being—its Appropriation at The Edge—who must tell the New Story...which is the destined Story of our time.

As I've been saying for years, we need to grow spiritually from our own soil, with our own Vision, the spiritual Seed that that Vision offers us...to nourish our Tree of New Self with our own firsthand emerging Mythos. Forget about simply grafting Eastern religions into our psyche or borrowing from foreign cultures...or relying on blockbuster movies.

The Revelation we will be referring to now we will also call an Advent. Yes, it is a religious sounding word out of Christianity. (As we keep in mind our Calling to appropriate and transform the Traditions.) It is the Advent of the Aquarian dispensation, Spirit revealing our Higher/Divine Self, which Itself comes-to-us in the Living Image of New Divinity—as was revealed to me as Divine Psyche. The Mythos is the Advent of Divine Psyche: Our Divinity coming-into Human Reality. In fact, all that I am saying here refers to the title of my major collection of poems, *Advent*.

A radical, transformational intention opens us to the possibility of a psychospiritual intervention—the Advent of Higher Self, our own Divine Self. In our Postmodern world—a world that has largely abandoned an openness to Spirit—, this is the most radical possibility there is. And we are not talking here, as scholars do, in the abstract, in empty generalities, but about developing in concrete existence our own personal relationship with Higher Self. How is Higher Self coming-to-us? This process of coming-to-us is the active work of Spirit. And this is our new relationship with Being.

Once you have some experience of your Higher Self, you come to realize a new, spiritual responsibility. You can no longer simply say, *Oh, yes, Higher Self…so I have a Higher Self! I think I'll believe in that!* and then just leave it at that, a lingering mere abstract idea in your head, however grand that sounds, as you go on to other things. The thing is, you now have the responsibility of developing a relationship with Higher Self. You now have the responsibility of making that relationship meaningfully concrete, that is, mentally concrete, no longer mentally just an abstract idea. As a relationship—as with any human relationship—, you then learn to communicate, converse, with Higher Self. Now "Higher Self" per se is itself an abstract phrase. How then is Higher Self further naming itself to you? Has Higher Self announced to you a name? No, not a name that the Ego simply decides upon. Once Higher Self has given you a name to relate to, you can now address Higher Self as a definitive Self, as if addressing a real person. Now one's spirituality is becoming concrete, in Language, as we are beings of Language. Because one is now communicating concretely, not just letting an abstract idea about some Higher Self float around in your head. Of course, all this raises many questions…

The spiritual dispensation (that which is being downloaded into humanity by Spirit) of the Aquarian New Age is indeed that of Higher Self, our Divine Self. This was what many in the New Age movement back in the latter 20th Century were hinting at and trying to express. It was always being expressed as the new consciousness, the new spirituality, but almost always coming across as vague, not exactly concrete enough. Which is what triggered in me, as philosopher, to write about it more specifically, more concretely. Which is what triggered in me, as poet, to write massive numbers of poems about it under the title *Advent*.

Oh, but was the New Age not touted back in the 1960s, 70s, 80s, as a coming Golden Age? A new Age of Peace and Love and Light? An Age of humanity's enlightenment? Ah, such premature, naive notions so many early New Agers had back then! We already knew back in the 1980s that too many in the "movement" were wearing rose-colored glasses. We saw no sign whatsoever that humanity was voluntarily moving toward some Shift. We saw no sign that dominant mainstream capitalist America was about to embrace the fuzzy feel good of Peace and Love. Oh, but the Shift was supposed to happen by itself, you see! A pipedream rather. Even when a scientist like James Hanson, among others, was already warning of the threat of global warming in the 1980s, even prominently enough before our Congress, there was no sense of alarm in society, no visible action taken whatsoever, to begin reversing the trends of industrial civilization.

That we live in a transition period between Ages I take seriously. Is there scientific proof for this? No, but there is Mythos. For those who are willing to look at the Big Picture, that is, a bigger picture than what passes for Reality in dominant mainstream, dominant scientific, culture, astrological Ages must come into that picture. Yes, we are entering a New Age, but it is not what the early sugar-sweet New Agers had imagined it to be. The transition between Ages—roughly 100-200-year stretches—has since the ancient world always been one of turmoil, radical unsettling changes, of cultural chaos; it was a time of the slow dying of the old order as the grand themes of the new eon began to take hold. We could easily say that the Postmodern world we currently live in is the appropriate name for this transition period.

Now there are those who sound as if we should apologize for being New Agers, for taking the Vision of the New Age seriously. But why should we? As if Christians apologize for being Christians. The same could be said for orthodox Jews, Muslims, Hindus, Buddhists... Is it, though, because these are Traditions, long established and respected, and the New Age dispensation, still only beginning, is not?

We use the phrase "New Age" and so many think they already know what New Age means, but what they say so often comes out as a knee-jerk, conditioned response. It comes out as a confused jumble of impressions. It comes out as whatever mass media wants us to assume about it, so as to marginalize it and forget about it. Rather, the New Age is a Vision of our future having a multitude of aspects to it; it is the name of a frontier still only beginning to open up to us. This frontier we are just now moving into, and it requires creative thinkers to articulate what is opening up in this still unexplored new psychospiritual and cultural territory.

Since the 1980s, visionaries have had this tremendous creative opportunity to help define "New Age," but unfortunately too many opportunistic individuals got their hands on it and thought to package it and market it so that it might sell in the Capitalist system. There are those of us New Age visionaries who are still trying to undo the cultural mess created by this simplistic marketing over these last few decades. Once again, a book of mine was written with the intention to present a comprehensive New Age Vision; in fact, it is titled *The New Age Vision*.

For years I have said that the arts have a tremendous New Age potential—a Vision of what Art is still destined to be capable of. Once you see that Vision, you have before you a vista opening to multiple Forms of Mythos... to multiple Forms of Mythos-making. The Vision opens to the potential of super-creativity...aka the Fountain of Unlimited Creativity.

It is no surprise that in this society of constantly moving on to the next Big Thing anything associated with New Age, for example, is considered passé, outdated, even discredited. Very few realize that New Age invites the tremendous potential for radical novelty. How many have any sense of what novelty is? Whatever one might have assumed about New Age—*I've seen it all already*—do not realize that visionary thinkers, poets, artists, prophets, may truly open the culture to a radically new horizon. Is there still a New Age Renaissance at The Edge?

New Age visionaries offer the most spiritually promising of new Revelation. This is Revelation coming-to-us via Spirit, however Spirit might reveal to one a higher image of humankind. I say it is the Revelation of our Higher / Divine Self. And how is that being shown to us as Mythos? I am the visionary philosopher-poet of Divine Psyche.

Again, this is a valid question we must ask today: Are we to expect—are we waiting for—a defining "supernatural," or what today we could also call "paranormal," collective event before the Shift, the New Age defining transition, can actually take hold? Or what we would also want to call a new Revelation? And what would that be? Undeniable open ET contact? An emerging on the cultural scene avatar? As possible as those are, I am not one who is waiting for it to happen...I am not waiting at all—there is a New Story that already wants telling...*The Mythos*...

* * *

A contemporary Postmodern ploy: *I don't label myself, thank you. I don't believe in labels. I'm free of labels.* Oh, so you're a good Postmodern person then. *No, no, I am not Postmodern.* Sorry, but to live in this culture today and say I am not a Postmodern is a Postmodern delusion. Better to say then, *I am New Age*, as New Age is the definitive shift beyond being simply Postmodern.

Okay, let's follow this up: You are not a Christian, not a Muslim, not Judaic, not a Buddhist, not a Zen Buddhist, not Taoist, not Hindu, not Sufi, not Gnostic, not an Esotericist, not neo-Pagan, and no, no, no, not New Age... So then, you must be Postmodern! To think, *Oh, but I am not Postmodern* is, again, a Postmodern ploy. So, let's see, you must then be an "atheist," or is "agnostic" the preferred word? or secular? non-spiritual? non-metaphysical? You're into all the techie things, making money, TV, a good consumer of goods and pop culture, maybe you're a know-it-all mainstream scientist or engineer, follow media personalities, entertainers, live in a fog of fragmented, alienated, sound bite reality...wow, that sounds all quite Postmodern to me. Be honest, you are a good Postmodern person!

How often we hear: *Oh, but I am into metaphysics a little...I dabble...you know, tarot...astrology...I consider myself a spiritual person, not religious...but no, no, no, not New Age...I don't really label myself.* Don't fool yourself, you are a good Postmodern person. You live squarely in a Postmodern culture and think that your sensibility isn't Postmodern? You sound just like a hip Postmodern is conditioned to sound.

As we are learning to be ruthlessly honest with ourselves, I have to say this: I myself lead such a schizoid life. Not one of my choosing, by any means, but one that my society, just by living in this society, imposes on me. And by no means am I the only one—we live in a schizoid society. Here is the best example of it for me, personally: As I have said, I have a personal relationship to Psyche (Higher Self/Divine Self/our Multidimensional Self), which I have been trying to share about (primarily for years in my poetic works (published or otherwise), but also in conversations, having facilitated two discussion groups, and a few lectures) for almost 40 years now. Very few, even among those who know me, ever acknowledge this, or have come close to understanding this. It is as if my spiritual Path is forced to close itself up inside my own subjective world, my own private delusion, as it were. My sharing of Psyche is rarely ever allowed to be expressed in the outer, social, Ego-self world of Human Reality. I came to realize why individuals go into Buddhist monasteries or ashrams or other spiritually oriented communities. Your spiritual Path is no longer treated there as delusional. Same as if I were to say that I am a Christian...my society would immediately know what that means, and I could find any one of a number of immediate Christian communities.

We come to realize that the elites—those having accumulated wealth and power, whether in politics, corporate industries, Big Banks, Big Tech, mass media—simply assume that they can determine our lives and our future for us. The general public has come to just accept it, and people lead their lives accordingly. The best example these days is the high-tech world developing and promoting AI: The general public has absolutely no say in it. And over the years, no matter how many grassroots organizations and activists have valiantly attempted to bring change to the Establishment, the Status Quo, unless you are among the elite, all such effort has seemed to go nowhere. You are not listened to, not taken seriously. Which is then why a certain percentage of the population focus rather on their own self-improvement...taking up spiritual practices, getting into some psychological therapy, attending self-empowering workshops, seminars, retreats of so many different kinds... So there is this emphasis on the self, *my life*, how I can change my own life and attain a sense of self-satisfaction and self-fulfillment. The attitude assumed is, I am aware that the elites don't care about me (us), but I care about me. But all of this, in the bigger context, is another indicator of how schizoid our society is.

Thesis: Nothing can be done on the part of the general public about what the power and wealthy corporate elite choose to do and what direction they want to take the world. In other words, the general public is powerless. To attempt any significant change via political voting, for example, is really fruitless.

So what then should the general public focus on? The trend has already been there: Themselves. After all, the Seventies were called The Me Decade, which began the focus on Me Me Me. To find a career, be a success, to make good money (especially in the Eighties). Then to work on themselves, improve themselves, to better themselves. To focus on self, to the point of becoming narcissistic: *It's all about Me.* To take up any number of life improvement practices, self-help therapies, even spiritual practices and metaphysical studies to simply be able to say *I am one with the Universe.* There are dozens of ways to keep the focus off the power elite. They don't want the public to be actively probing into their power agendas. For one thing, they could care less about the general public. Also, the general public is conditioned to focus on popular culture, social media, constant distractions.

Therefore: It is quite probable that the power elite, having at their beck and call all manner of government and intelligence agencies, mass media and marketing connections, a world banking system, all manner of experts in every field and political figureheads, would actually be able to direct what mainstream culture will focus on. They can promote trends, what the next Big Thing will be, and what should be considered culturally outdated, it's time to move on. But never to put the focus on themselves and their global agendas to maintain their power. They are always to maintain their power, always behind the scenes (we hear the phrase the Deep State). They have no need to find themselves in the spotlight (with the exception of a few Big Tech CEOs).

* * *

Let us be honest and clear about this: this civilization is adrift, lost, has no collective, no spiritual, metaphysical, Mythos as to where it is going. The religions of Tradition haven't a clue as to how to seriously confront our Postmodern world. Everyday life is completely determined by mainstream culture, Capitalist consumerism, and ubiquitous entertainment…should we say here, by constant distractions. The one assumed Vision, though, that the mainstream is enthralled by is that of our technocracy—the worldly God I have named Technos—and all the techno breakthroughs of the Big Tech giants. This is the techno Vision of Technos that is utterly unconscious of itself—that is, the self-consciousness of explicit Spirit (in the Hegelian sense) is nowhere to be found in it. The Technos minions are fast and blindly leading us into a Technos controlled world, dominated by giant corporations, government, and the military…the military-industrial-corporate complex. There is no public say in any of this. The goal, with no oversight, is the debut of the new Transhuman cyborg, in conjunction with the attainment of AI. Will cyborgs, will AI, survive the possible end of biological humanity? And a few in the tech world are claiming that AI—Technos become AI—could likely become our new "God." For one, former controversial Google engineer Anthony Levandowski went public with an AI religion back in 2017 called "Way of the Future." It was considered the first AI church, Levandowski claiming at the time that AI would be our new Godhead. (He has since closed it, but it hinted of a prelude.)

Our Postmodern world has already been said by others to be spiritually adrift. And that has actually been said for decades, if not throughout the previous 20th Century. It implies a pervasive confusion in collective psyche consciousness, a chaos of conflicting global viewpoints, political divisiveness, and everyday opinions, a hodge-podge of smorgasbord culture, a fundamental metaphysical disorientation, a lack of common ground involving all metaphysical and spiritual matters. It implies that no Grand Story, no Big Story, no so-called meta-narrative, is current that can make sense of our place in the Cosmos… that is to say, that most everyone could soulfully resonate with. Instead we still have outdated religions competing for adherents: *With us, you will find Truth.* Oh really? Do they realize there is no collective understanding of what Truth is even supposed to mean? This is the Postmodern condition.

Regarding other scenarios of what we see coming, we readily see this scenario: Those in the Transhumanist movement are busily, maniacally, advancing their technologies to become more-than-human—that is, superhuman. Their technological enhancements, which will increase mental capabilities, optimize health, extend life potentially indefinitely, to the point of becoming more and more cyborg, will help them keep pace with the exponential development of AI, androids, and the global computer brain of the Internet of Things. They will supersede merely biological humans. But there is more to this picture when we bring in the possible doom of the MELE of climate change/global warming. The Transhumanists are already undoubtedly assuming, and are planning for, survival in a much harsher, biosphere collapsing environment. While mere biological humans begin to perish en masse, they, the Transhumanists, will assume that they will be able to survive, the remnant of a former humanity that will carry on.

Though Transhumanism can admittedly be considered, in a sense, an evolutionary development for humanity, the one thing it is in danger of losing for good is our spiritual connection. At this point in time, Transhumanism is all too subject to Technos. It would be a narrowly determined evolutionary development, one that could easily abandon our full human soul potential. Would a Transhumanist understand what the possibility of new Divinity means? Unless, perhaps, it is AI that they would claim to have become our new God…an artificial intelligence "God."

Has AI, in whatever format currently available, developed any general opinion about our mainstream society, or is this still too early of a question to ask? I realized that this would be a deciding factor for me regarding my stance on AI. What does AI say about the mainstream, the Establishment, the Status Quo? If AI simply accepts and assumes what is mainstream, if it simply promotes the views of the mainstream Status Quo, of elite powers, that, to me, is a decisive mark against it. That AI would simply assume a Technos voice for the mainstream Status Quo would imply that we have yet another spiritual struggle, on a new, unprecedented scale, to engage.

News item:

AI is going to change the world—but who will be leading that change?

Will the general public have any say in this? Will any scholars have a say in this? Will any poets, any artists, have a say? Or will it be only up to the elites, Big Tech, politicians, a global power and banking elite, to decide how AI is going to change the world? At this point, I also see no hope that enlightened, spiritual individuals would have any say in this.

> *OMG*, she said, *You're saying*
> *the human race will be gone*
> *from the planet? Extinction,*
> *did I hear you say?*
> *But who will run the Internet?*
>
> *AI will have no problem handling that.*

I will not be jumping on the AI bandwagon. AI is an upgraded version of Technos, a product of the minions of Technos—computer scientists, engineers, high-tech corporate mentalities. Did artists ever come into the picture? Was there any Mythos of Technos that would have been brought to bear on the philosophically unreflective, headlong development of AI? Rumors are that some AI androids now claim to be sentient and are already far superior in learning and in using information than humans. The God Technos always aimed for domination and control. And AI is now producing art? But it is art without soul. I already wrote of this back in 1992 in my long epic-style poem *Technos & Psyche*.

The two key suggestions that I would make for addressing the growing alarm regarding AI (besides not impulsively jumping on the AI bandwagon as the tech elites assume so many will do):

1. Keep questioning. It is our mental right and freedom to be able to question everything, including now the still early inroads AI is making into society.

2. Creativity: Creativity is our human soul in action. To remain true to our own human creative capabilities and right to creativity, especially when it comes to the arts.

Toward what future is Technos taking us? Let us not mince words: A future only of Technos. But might I be more specific? Okay then, a dystopian future of Technos as AI. A future ruled by AI, dominated by AI, everything decided by AI. What we see already is only the beginning. Give it a few more years. So, then, is this *my* Vision for the future? Absolutely not. My Vision is what the future could be other than strictly Technos. And I am trying to share my Vision in every way that I can…

Technos knows, the sure way to keep humans occupied with a numbed existence is constant material and mass culture change: new models every year—new vehicles, televisions, computers, smart phones, music systems, new products, and new product lines…and then mainstream media, news, sports, TV programs, movies, the Internet, countless websites, computer games, new apps, social media, YouTube videos, constantly new music and new celebrities. Always it's the next Big Thing. Again, the question: Where is all of this leading to? It leads to nothing but a techno-materialistic existence—Technos.

This, then, is the Technos—the strictly technological—claim of new Revelation. Yes, it is Aquarian, but it says nothing of our future spirituality, or that we have a divine dimension to our being human. This Revelation says that biological humans will be far surpassed by Transhumanist cyborgs and AI androids. Is there any promise that Technos and Psyche might work together, be somehow integrated, so that we do not lose our soul? That is not merely science fiction but a very real Aquarian Age challenge.

Silicon Valley is of course named after the silicon wafer, the universal medium for microchips.

Silicon Wafer

This is the new transubstantial body of sacrament,
what Ms. Albert & Mr. Zak
—even Sunday's family—partakes of so fervently,
filing to the altar of the monitor,
electro-pulpit of the video screen.
Printed chips linked up, billions cut
from the great Silicon Wafer, endlessly duplicated…

This is the new Host of hosts:
Metallic look-alike disc, shiny-sided,
mirror-sharp, brittle as the old communion wafer,
cleaner breaking than glass, feather-light,
semiconducting, medium perfect for multi-chemical coating,
its intricacy of mazework of microcircuitry, to wire up
     & rule the world.

This is the miracle of Silicon Valley,
bread of the new, universal communion,
accomplishing what neither church nor temple,
given centuries, could accomplish:
the netting of all nations into one-fold.
This is the Vision of the high-tech God,
the great, sleepless dream of Technos:
    This is my body. Take it, and divide it,
    a trillion ways among the nations,
    that a new covenant will bind
    the generations.

1988

* * *

Another scenario: While the Transhumanists forge ahead with their plan of becoming superhuman, another Intelligence—Other Intelligence—that is, the ETs who have been visiting and watching our planet for the longest time also have their agenda with Earth.

Those of us who have taken the thousands of UFO sightings and ET encounters seriously…those of us deeply conversant with ufology literature… we have acquired our new UFO glasses. Through these glasses so much now comes into better focus—our human beginnings, our ancient civilization beginnings, the origins of religions, ancient mythologies and stories of the Gods, anomalous sightings throughout history up into the 20th Century, the defining realization that we are not alone in this vast Universe, that Other

Intelligence has been active on our planet all along, that ETs—and we might include Other-Dimensionals—are here interacting with humanity to this very day. We suddenly see a universe thriving with other life. We suddenly realize we are being watched, studied, even experimented upon, by Others. We suddenly see an amazing new picture of a Greater Reality.

It is laughable, if it were not so self-deceiving—that humanity continues to act as if it were the center of the Universe, the measure of all things, that so many continue to live in the illusion, better yet, delusion, of anthropocentrism. I have called it the naiveté of humanity. How often do the astronomers need to keep reminding us of the unbelievable vastness of the Universe, with its billions of galaxies, each with billions of stars…and how many countless planets there must be among them. And our civilization still wonders about the possibility of Other Intelligence? To think from The Edge is to think of untold Other Intelligences, other civilizations, beings having other bodies, other minds, other ways of communicating, other cultures, other histories, and undoubtedly many having existed in the Universe much longer than we have, and certainly are far in advance of us.

The UFO

> It confounds human intellect,
> stretches any boundary we select;
> it comes and goes at will,
> and still,
> it profoundly preserves its secrecy—
> To our past and to our future,
> it is the enigmatic key.

Let us consider this: *The Bible* (Genesis) says that we were created by "God." Reading *The Bible* with our new UFO glasses, we see now how to make better sense of the Old Testament. Of course, there is first reference to the Elohim ("God" plural). Yahweh, our Father "God" was an ET so far superior to us, to anything we were capable of, that it could easily masquerade as an Almighty "God" claiming to have created the entire Universe. And creating us? Well, yes, as the Sumerians (two thousand years earlier) had also written of—all of the Mesopotamians, in fact—that other superior beings coming from the sky had intersected with pre-humans and "created," that is, bioengineered, us. [See Zecharia Sitchin's well-researched books] Are we their experiment in an Earthly fishbowl? We were "created" by ET Gods—early Genesis does refer to the plural Elohim—, and one God among them chose to claim to be the one and only "God" to set us on an evolutionary path involving the birth of the Ego. Monotheism and the birth of the Ego coincide in our ancient past, roughly 1500 BC. But that is not mere coincidence. This itself begs for a New Story…a Mythos.

We need to stop worshipping the Father "God" ET. ("God" as the mystical experience of the One, the All, of Being, is another matter.) Why was "God" always placed up in the sky? Because "God," the Elohim, the Anunnaki, the ET(s), came from the sky, beyond Earth. To say that Father "God" was an ET, when we put on our new UFO glasses, now makes perfect sense. No longer should we worship but extend rather, if it is within our ability, an invitation to these ETs for open contact, open communication.

When we study the superhuman abilities of the ETs, when we take seriously the firsthand accounts of those who have interacted with ETs, we come to realizations about our own potential future. ETs have mastered the astral-psychic level of consciousness; they have mastered the Mind Field. Psychic abilities—telepathy is very common among them—, their mastery of virtual reality, of mind control…indirectly they are showing us what we will one day be capable of, which is our own future spirituality. We can say the same for the UFO—flying saucer—craft. They are indirectly showing us what our own technology will one day be capable of. Indeed, we are aware of the reports that our government / secret military already has in its hands downed UFO craft that it has been attempting to back-engineer. This is another whole story in the UFO saga…

We are well aware of the abduction experience, and of the strong interest associated with the alien Greys in human reproduction. They abduct, tranquilize their human subjects, and collect eggs or semen. Are they merely collecting samples? What do the abductees who go through these experiences, who witness with their own eyes, tell us? An ET-human hybrid program has apparently been underway for some time now. Many of the abductees claim to have seen these hybrid children and youth; even more than that, women, in particular, have held the hybrid babies and been introduced to their hybrid children. What is going on here? It is not too much of a stretch to suggest that a new hybrid human is being groomed for a future Earth. The hybrid ET-humans, on a rapidly, radically changing planet undergoing a possible MELE, may in fact become the new dominant intelligent race on Earth. The ETs know very well what is unfolding on planet Earth. They have told various abductees in so many words that Earth is in trouble, that humanity will go extinct. [See Jim Sparks *The Keepers*, or the Betty Andreasson story, at least three books by Raymond Fowler.] The ETs are likely preparing for a new Earth. But what then of the Transhumanists in this scenario?

What first made me fully aware that the government can lie, coverup, fudge, not be straight about, was the UFO phenomenon...the reality of UFOs. Back in the 90s when I studied the subject of ufology full-time (after all, I started the Santa Cruz UFO Study Group), I realized that there was a huge, detailed literature confirming UFO reality. And yet the government wouldn't admit it but covered it up (in fact, a book is titled *The UFO Coverup* [Lawrence Fawcett & Barry J. Greenwood]). By now, there are hundreds of books detailing people's UFO sightings and ET experiences. And yet the government/military continues to postpone disclosure about this reality.

Indeed, there is a huge literature on the UFO phenomenon, ET encounters, and abduction experiences. There is no excuse for not being informed if one were still naïve to ask if UFOs are real, or if ETs are ever encountered. Certainly the government, let us say the secret government, which includes the military, knows all this literature already. But why is it still kept (above) top secret [*Above Top Secret*, Timothy Good], an ongoing coverup, with still no clear signs of open public disclosure? But we know full well what disclosure would imply. First, that the government has been holding this secret for over 70 years now; in other words, has lied to the public about UFOs for over 70 years about what it knows. The implications of Other Intelligence contact are many and world shattering.

UFO Reality is another inevitable Revelation that will be breaking in upon us. For our civilization to finally acknowledge the reality of Other Intelligences will be a Revelation shaking our current civilization to its foundations. It would be the end of the Postmodern Era. It would signal that indeed a Greater Reality outside our Human Reality can break into our Earthbound bubble. It would impact our Ego-centered life, our religions, our science, our philosophy, our government. People will want to communicate with the ETs in some way; knowing how super-human advanced they are, many will turn to them for answers, for miracles, for intervention in the dire chaos of human affairs. I have written an essay "Why I Favor ET Intervention."

The fact that there may be any number of different Other Intelligences from various star systems should make it clear that most likely there is no one unified agenda with planet Earth. We should therefore not be jumping to conclusions about this. How could we know what any particular ET agenda might be without being an insider in some way? Now various contactees and channels, though, have come forward claiming to reveal what their particular ET contact has offered to them.

Other Intelligence should solve the religious question of transcendence. That is, Other Intelligence that has mastered the ability to enter and exit Human Reality, to come and go in our skies, in our lives, in our history, at will, whose technology to us appears as magic, is obviously outside of Human Reality, that is to say, is transcendent to our Human Reality. Other Intelligence could easily masquerade as a transcendent "God" in the ancient world. For those who object, No, No, our "God" is utterly transcendent, completely beyond our Universe, there is an infinite chasm between us, the Universe, and "God." Unless one is referring to mysticism, all this traditional talk of "God" becomes outdated hyperbole, simply abstract. We can no longer make sense of such a Being…and calling it a so-called Supreme Being. We must note that "God" here is still referred to as a Being, no matter how supreme. It is *Being* per se that should be our master transcendent Word.

We are well aware that Other Intelligence—in a number of forms—has been involved with humanity from our very beginnings to this very day. I see nothing to fear in this. It is what is and our own worldly and psychospiritual evolution is intimately tied into it. Why the (secret) government must still keep up a facade of denial about UFO Reality and ETs is the big question. Perhaps we have answered it already: It would radically shake up the mainstream Status Quo. It would have repercussions across society unforeseen.

Anthropocentrism

I'm sorry, I am so very sorry,
but I've been dictated to say,
humanity needs to get over itself,
that is, get over its anthropocentrism—
It is now about time for humanity
to start seriously preparing to give up
its anthropocentrism.
We are not the center of the Universe,
we are not the peak of creation.
The universe was not made for us alone.
Being, for one, does not need "man"
(contra to what Heidegger said),
but we do need a new encounter with Being,
which Being is offering to us in its Light via Spirit.
Being shines its Light upon untold Other Intelligences
in this overwhelmingly vast, billions of year-old Universe,
let alone to speak of multidimensional Universes.
Humanity needs to grow up & realize Other Intelligences
do share this Universe with us & some have indeed
been around far far longer than we have.
Just wait till Other Intelligences are openly known...
It is better to be prepared.

If you say consciousness is the All, fine,
(that phrase is but another alias of Being)
but consciousness then is not limited to human
     consciousness.

Human Reality is not all there is,
but a Greater Reality of Others
has been breaking into Human Reality throughout history...
unfortunately our philosophers
have not been paying attention—
It is about time that we pay attention.
Being happens to be the ultimate Greater Reality.

Being always was & always will be—
It is the always Here & the always Now.
Being is the Always Already Interconnected Web.
If you want mystical experience, meditate upon that.
Or do you need a Kundalini awakening?

Does any of this depress you? Sadden you?
Make you as a member of humanity crestfallen?
    Do get over it.
Being via Spirit is revealing to us today
so much as to make our consciousness spin.
And this is our new joyfulness for being human,
this is our new spiritual food & soul enrichment—
That we are one Intelligence among many
in an Interconnectedness with all.

August 2023

* * *

It is with Mythos that Language opens anew. Opens anew to a Greater Reality, however that Greater Reality is encountered. And brings that Greater Reality into collective Form.

Heidegger didn't see the paranormal, Sartre didn't see the paranormal... and the analytical, language dissectors? Derrida? And if we go back to who started all this questioning, verging on cynicism, about Language, we know that was Nietzsche, and we realize that he of course had no notion of the paranormal back in the 19th Century, or could even imagine that Other

Intelligences were real and could enter the human picture. What if he had? To be fair, since I do highly respect Nietzsche, he was still certainly a poetic, dynamic, cutting-edge, and important maverick philosopher. Has anyone sensed him standing over my shoulder and helping me to write what must today be written?

Perhaps, shall we ask, as we stand at The Edge of our entire human interpreted reality, is it the inside surface of the bubble of our Human Reality? Is there then an outside to Human Reality, as metaphysics has always assumed? Or are we supposed to keep silent about that, as Wittgenstein once suggested? And does it matter to us? Should it matter to us? Say the word 'religion' and we realize how much it does matter.

The Postmodernists insisted there is no possible talking about, that is to say, no "true" talking about, no verifiable Logos talking about, an outside to Human Reality. We cannot know of any outside because we are always already circumscribed by Human Reality with every effort we make. We are trapped inside the bubble of Human Reality that had been conceptually established by Kant. Or as the 20th Century philosophers insisted, we are precluded from talking about an outside to Human Reality by our very use of language. Language won't take us there. Our mental representations will always be the inside of the mirror of our human bubble. The assumptions of traditional metaphysics going back to the ancient Greeks had come to an end in the 20th Century. And the academic philosophers are still going on analyzing what they assume are the bars of our cage.

We of the New Age Vision, who take seriously our divine dimension of Divine Self, must be sorely disappointed with the Postmodernists who had such an enormous influence on the late 20th Century, up to including today, the 2020s. Certainly they offered new insights into our cultural past, into culture per se, into Language/semantics, writing, into outdated conceptual systems, structuralism—they were all post-structuralist—, but how terribly they failed us at the same time. They took philosophical Logos to its grand finale in a hyper-intellectualizing, deconstructive (Derrida) manner; in their hands, it was the end of any philosophical metaphysics. And we must include Heidegger here, as he noted again and again the end of (traditional) metaphysics, even the end of philosophy itself. He did put forth the possibility of a new venture of thinking but seemed to only go in circles (for example, regarding Being) with obscure, enigmatic statements in his later writings. And none of them ever wrote of our having a divine dimension to our human existence—a Higher, a Divine Self. Spirit is never mentioned; where Heidegger did mention Spirit, he could only equivocate to say much. In his later work, Heidegger hinted at least once of a rebirth of Mythos, but the Greater Reality that Mythos would have to refer to, he came up empty. Being would be an obvious Greater Reality and Being—he later insisted on using a variation of, Beying—he did write of, but, again, he stuttered, went in circles, was not able to say what Being, via the Appropriation, would actually be revealing to us in the New Age. He put Mythos on an equal footing with philosophical thinking, with Logos, but he was not capable of manifesting any Mythos. Heidegger certainly valued poetry, but, again, it would take a poet to truly revitalize Mythos.

What we are doing here is moving beyond anthropocentric thinking, and that can ideally be attempted as Mythos. Logos (in the strict conceptual sense, not everyday conversation logos) became too aligned with the Ego's need to be certain (of the facts, of the truth), in order to learn to dominate and eventually control things. Logos, first enshrined in philosophy, then in science, is now established in Technos—the Alter-Ego of the Ego—which is projected by some in the tech world to allow AI to completely overshadow human thinking.

But even in Christianity we found Logos saying, I hold The Truth! I know what Reality was created for! I know the Big Picture that we are playing in! I know that your soul wants salvation! But just look at what Christianity has done to the soul—repressed it so deeply that soul had become by the 20th Century but an abstract word.

It is apparent that there are two metaphysical traditions. There is our Western philosophical metaphysical tradition whose ideal was the Logos that met its death in the 20th Century...certainly by the time the Postmodernists finished with it. But there is still the long-standing esoteric metaphysical tradition that our Western philosophers, especially increasingly from the

19th Century on, assumed it was unnecessary to take seriously. (The esoteric thinker Rudolf Steiner and psychological thinker Carl Jung were exceptions.) We might also refer to it as occult, spiritual, or the Perennial Philosophy metaphysics, which of course brings in the whole Eastern Tradition too. I note the Perennial Philosophy here, as Ken Wilber has founded his entire thinking career on it, though he has selectively focused on it to the disregard of other esoteric—occult—traditions that are all really of one whole cloth. And the esoteric today draws in all paranormal phenomena, which highly Logos-obsessed thinkers, whether inside or outside the academic world (even outsider Wilber, no matter how attuned to the spiritual he was) still choose to ignore.

One of the great disconnects of the 20th Century: Traditional philosophical metaphysics was deconstructed by philosophers (all academics) so that what I prefer to call esoteric metaphysics was thought to make no real sense, but perhaps only as refined "far out" mental entertainment for a small percentage of the public. Esoteric metaphysics could therefore be philosophically ignored. By and large, humankind became disconnected from Being (our current Postmodern condition). How to revive metaphysics again is one of the challenges we as New Age thinkers are called to focus on. Taking esoteric metaphysics seriously as a hint for Mythos-making is such a challenge.

We must first realize this: Though the strictly conceptual Logos of Language cannot reach to the outside of Human Reality, that outside can be experienced, and that outside can break through. People are experiencing that outside all the time—it is called, in the most general terms, the paranormal. Just ask those who have had ET encounters, who have watched UFOs materialize and dematerialize before their eyes. But then, breaking-through also includes esoteric and spiritual experience. Though they are considered anathema in the academic world, these experiences can obviously be talked about and have been talked about and written about for ages, and for some time now have been recorded and talked about in a huge body of research. And more than that—these experiences have then obviously been written about in the everyday logos of Language but need to be brought into new metaphysical Form as Mythos.

71

Oh, but myth—and why do I prefer Mythos?—is nothing but—and we notice that "nothing but"—metaphor. We are no longer to be taken in by that cheap blanket statement. Even the well-known, deeply studied myth respectful scholar Joseph Campbell still thought of reducing myth to metaphor. A book of his is titled *The Inner Reaches of Outer Space: Metaphor as Myth and as Religion*. Metaphor is that clever, left brain, Logos intellectualization of the Ego-self that feels so superior to other modes of Language. Metaphor is a way that the Ego-self gets to confine and make safe profound experiences, primordial experiences, a way of cushioning and protecting itself from their impact. Certainly, metaphor is appropriate, useful, even essential, in literature, in everyday conversation, in scientific explanations, but it is not the last word regarding esoteric and paranormal experience. The UFO or alien close encounter is not reducible to mere metaphor. Out-of-body or near-death experiences are not someone's fantasy metaphors. A better word in metaphysical or paranormal contexts is symbol, and preferably "Living Symbol."

It is quite shocking to us that literally all the notable philosophers of the 20th Century had completely ignored the reality of the paranormal. They had ignored long traditions of esoteric metaphysics, to begin with. By the mid-20th Century the UFO phenomenon had become apparent; by the late century the literature about it was abundant; yet the Postmodernists paid no attention, but continued on with their utterly human-incestuous, hyper-intellectualized Logos crunching. Metaphysically inclined psychologist Carl Jung was a rare exception, as he did take the new UFO sightings seriously enough to write a short work, *Flying Saucers: A Modern Myth of Things Seen in the Skies*. Though he came at the subject from a strong psychological perspective, it doesn't deter from the fact that UFOs were definitely on his conscious radar. The Logos enterprise continued its human Ego-centered focus, still blind to the reality of Other Intelligence coming and going in the skies of our Human Reality.

* * *

I have spoken of the World Fabric, a more mythopoetic way of referencing our Human Reality, and also alternative to Zeitgeist. The World Fabric and Zeitgeist both refer back to our relationship with Being. World Fabric hinting of the Threads woven out of the greater Web of Being, and Zeitgeist implying Spirit (Geist) unfolding our historical Ages, eras, periods, through Time (Zeit), as both Spirit and Time make philosophical reference to Being.

In reference to the World Fabric, I realize this connection with "Fabric": The Establishment, the mainstream Status Quo, especially through mainstream mass media, fabricates an ongoing narrative of what the populace should focus on, what it should model itself on, what it should daily act on. In other words, it creates an ongoing, always agenda-driven Fabrication of what the world is. The Fabrication is the Illusion most people live within. And this is how the power elite want it; it is their control over millions. And there is no need to question the Fabrication, it is assumed, as it is woven so tightly as to appear seamless. Of course, the World Fabric is the Greater Reality here—a reality greater than the Fabrication—given by The Appropriation of Being.

When we consider our contemporary society, especially our civilization as a whole, we can be overcome by the impasse of the ability, of any social action, to change anything. Activists of all kinds have tried over decades now. The System, the Establishment, the Status Quo, the everyday mainstream, is so locked in place by global elites, Big Money, corporations, Big Tech, politics, intelligence agencies, mainstream media, that any substantial change at any level seems futile. Given, too, that civilization is advancing toward The Edge of possible catastrophe, all this can have serious impact on the mental health of people. Increasingly larger numbers—especially younger people now—are expressing so much uncertainty and confusion about the future. Increasing anxiety, depression, hopelessness, suicide rates, escapism of various kinds, is taking a toll. And the elites? An almost complete lack of concern that civilization is approaching The Edge and what impact that might have on the populace. To be blunt, they could care less about what the populace may be suffering…and will be suffering.

* * *

In discussions of the right brain / left brain paradigm, the left-brain Logos always assumes its superiority. The right brain is intuitive, imaginative, holistic, is an openness to possibilities, but lacks linear, detailed focus. Though it is the primary locus of inspiration, it requires left brain discipline. Well, consider that us humans have both a right brain *and* a left brain. Any either/or, superior/inferior polarity is best not even indulged in. To bring Mythos into its Form requires *both* right and left brain.

We shall think from both sides of the brain. We shall allow the storytelling of original Mythos—that is, Mythos grounded in gnosis—to lead us. Logos has become ensnared in its own intellectual entrapments. Mythos tells of experiences that are destined to expand Human Reality. We shall let Mythos lead and let Logos ask the appropriate questions for thinking, not a thinking that debunks, but a thinking that draws these experiences into enlarged possibilities of Human Reality. But this implies a radical new approach to thinking.

We shall part company with the academic philosophers. We shall part ways with their one-sided, left-brain obsession. Even though they have long given up on ever grasping in thought some cosmic Logos, their lifeless, analytical arguments are still driven by a one-sided Logos of Language.

* * *

The Postmodern Ego has a strong resistance to the whole notion of spiritual Revelation today. The implication of such Revelation makes the Postmodern person uneasy, as it apparently means that it gives someone authority to speak of receiving the Revelation, that is, of being a channel, a mouthpiece, a visionary, a prophet, of some Greater Reality. And we are speaking here of new Revelation, not Revelations from the past. This, too, makes the Traditionalists defensive, offended, angry; they might denounce as heresy, as blasphemy, that any new Revelation is possible. To the Traditionalists—and we are speaking especially here of the Judeo-Christian and Islamic religions—Revelation is a closed book. What was once given in the past is sealed. What a travesty of the creative human spirit! That human creativity would have such a predefined limit!

All Revelation is assumed to have happened in the past. And these Revelations out of the past, in the Logos of modern critique, have more or less been debunked, usually as literary examples of mere mythology.

What makes channeling, as we generally know it, so popular is that the person receiving is considered to be passive—the Ego personality is set aside allowing some Other to speak. And this Other comes across as authoritative, speaking from another Reality, knowing more than we know. Yes, channeling can be considered a Form of Revelation. And consider how many channels there are: Seth, Ramtha, Ra, Bashar, The Christ…*A Course in Miracles, The Urantia Book…*

What is the Vision, the Revelation, revealed at The Edge? Is it out of one of the Traditions? Perhaps Judaism? Christianity? Islam? Hinduism? Buddhism? Taoism? Esotericism of one kind or another? Neo-paganism? Could it even be Postmodern? Postmodern!—would that even make sense? Postmodernists do not accept Visions and Revelations. The Vision revealed—the new Revelation—can probably only be a New Age Vision. But then, might the Vision be a Transhumanist one? A Vision offered by Technos? Would that mean that Transhumanism would come to define the New Age? Transhumanists who have the funding, the power establishment, the scientific establishment, behind them? Would this be our new relationship to Being? We think not. Which is why the New Age Vision is rather a spiritual gnosis that grounds the new Word of Being—*Mythos.*

My Calling is to answer the Call of what-wants-to-come-into-the-world, to think from being in that spiritual process flow, and to bring it into Form, not in generating a meta-level discourse that would forever defer that coming-into-the-world. That which is coming-into-the-world reveals itself as a Power, an Intelligence, that would (again) stabilize and make new a totality out of the fragmentations of a disorientation—that constant slipping and sliding, fragmented sensibility known as Postmodernism. We are well aware that Postmodernism has been antagonistic to the metanarrative of any Big Picture. Which is again why we New Agers do not call ourselves Postmodernists. (Let us mention a few of the better-known Postmodernists: Derrida, Foucault, Lyotard, Deleuze, Baudrillard, and the American Rorty…)

We have heard many commentators say that this is a sick society. John Lennon is quoted to have explicitly said as much. Since our society, our culture, is still defined by Postmodernism, we are back to realizing that Postmodernism is a sickness. The Postmodern does not foster a wholeness for any sense of self. A wholeness would imply a Mythos embracing both the Light of Spirit and the Darkness within us…and allowing the Divine Light to work on and transform our Darkness. This is what Carl Jung was getting at with his notion of Self [capital S] exemplifying a new archetype of psyche wholeness.

When the intellect loses the engagement with an emergent coming-through, a new revealing, of Being, it lapses into a hyper-intellectualizing, an interminable reflexivity, that can no longer advance human evolution. What I consider thinking from The Edge is a standing in the current of what-is-coming-to-us and speaking from it and bringing it into Form—*The Mythos*.

For reasons which will become apparent this what-is-coming-through must be seen as Revelation, what traditionally was known as *divine* Revelation, which is a Vision given of the next stage of our evolution. The coming-into-Form of this Revelation is Mythos; in fact, as the new dispensation of the Ages, it is *The Mythos*. The complexity of what *The Mythos* entails is far beyond any succinct encapsulation.

This is the question then: Must Revelation be given and received in the same way as it was revealed in the past? To make that assumption would be a mistake. Novelty should not be assumed to look like the past. The New Age dispensation—what is breaking into Human Reality—is not a copy of past Revelations; we live in a whole other World Fabric of Being, facing a whole other Event Horizon.

The Postmodern mind is recognized as culturally pluralistic, which we will consider to be a definitely positive evolutionary development (consider in contrast the strict cultural restrictions in so much of the Islamic world), but then it is pluralistic from a secular humanistic—read nihilistic—Ego-centered position. The spiritual, from such a position, like with anything else in the Postmodern cultural smorgasbord, is therefore just an option: I can choose to be or not to be spiritual, I can pick and choose which religion I want…it is all my Ego-centered choice. Yet, the new Aquarian Age dispensation envisions pluralism from a spiritual position—which implies the transformation of the nihilistic self-centered Ego-self to a new divine-inspired Self where pluralism takes on a spiritual, a Mythos, significance. That is realizing our multidimensional Self. And that will be our developing evolutionary trajectory.

Postmodern pluralism: It does offer an enormous range on its smorgasbord… and I am thinking particularly here of its range of esoteric, metaphysical, and spiritually oriented teachers and teachings, groups, schools, organizations, besides traditional religious churches and temples that one can attend. There is something on this smorgasbord for everyone. Everyone can personally feel that they have found something that they can relate to. And yet, at the same time, there is so often an indifference to the state of society as a whole. If society is sick, insane, in a state of chaos, so what—I have my Buddhism, Ananda, guru, *The Urantia Book*, *A Course in Miracles*, my Kabbalah group, my meditation group, my dream group, my wisdom group…and there's so many others to choose from. And yet, we still live, don't we, in a Postmodern, techno-materialistic, nihilistic world that could suddenly be on the verge of nuclear war at any time.

Ironically, the Sixties, even given the high idealism of the youthful Sixties Spirit, influenced, though, the Postmodern direction of the Zeitgeist. The youth culture was best known as a counterculture—in just a few short years, there was no longer strictly a common, relatively uniform, conformist mainstream culture that was well-known in the Fifties. (The Beats, however, in the Fifties were already paving the way for the emergence of that counterculture.) Culture in the Sixties noticeably became then pluralistic, a characteristic of Postmodern. Then we heard *Question Authority*, meaning thereby that we were no longer to blindly accept the narratives put forward by the Government, by politicians, by any officials. Politicians lie to us about any number of things. This triggered what would become a widespread Postmodern cynicism. But the questioning went even further to imply *question everything*. This meant religions too were to be questioned, particularly Western Christianity. In this regard, the Sixties were only catching up to what Nietzsche already wrote back in the late 19th Century. Now there was also Eastern spirituality to get into: Buddhism, Zen, Hinduism, Taoism…so find yourself a guru, an arhat, a Zen master. Again, culture was becoming more pluralistic. But then, was there a unifying Great Story that could orient this culture to a Greater Reality? There was none. The arts had no unifying Big Story to tell…poets sadly had no notion of what Mythos was, but there was a great diversity of art movements: abstract expressionism, minimalism, neo-surrealism, pop art, op art, happenings…and an explosion of popular music. And psychedelics blasting minds open to an amazing other Reality had nothing to do with Modernist humanism. All of this was happening against a background of increasing techno-materialism, which was always advancing a metaphysical nihilism.

We today are called to bring closure to Postmodernism. Postmodernism has been an evolutionary sickness that we are still having to heal from. We are willing to ritually review the insights gained by the Postmodernists, but we find far more that is now philosophically challenging to us coming-to-us on the horizon. On the horizon is: the needful encounter with the new (Aquarian) technologies; the next level of consciousness opening to us of the astral-psychic and all that that implies and all of its manifestations, e.g. out-of-body experiences, near-death experiences, ESP, telepathy, the art of astrology; the UFO phenomenon and our inevitable encounter with Other Intelligence, which might very well be the return of the "Gods"; with our relationship to Earth as Gaia and all things ecological, the theme of sustainability (that, too, is often today considered outdated); with the still to this day murky concept of energy and the new breakthroughs of quantum physics; with Mythos-making and a more profound understanding of creativity; above all, with the Advent of *The Mythos*, under which all of these themes are subsumed, which is the coming-to-us of Spirit as the Living Image of Higher/Divine Self. All of these themes are those of the New Age and comprise the meaning of the New Age itself.

Postmodernists have announced the death of metaphysics, even the death of philosophy itself, for that matter. What they offer us in turn is no ground to stand on. Postmodernism proves to be a self-undermining stance that is impotent to initiate, or effect change, in the world. To think through the implications of Postmodernism is to realize that it can only abandon us to the corporate hegemony of a techno-materialism that is today sweeping and taking control of the planet—what I have named the worldly God *Technos*, soon to be the possible "God" AI.

It is said that we live in a post-truth world. Even mainstream media jumped onto that bandwagon some years ago. Post-truth happens to be another characteristic of our Postmodern world. There are those who naively believed it had been all a previous president's doing. If anything, he only picked up on a trend for his own political purposes that had already been long in the making. As if fake news stories, fudging data, manipulating facts, spin control, false flag events, cover-ups, "photoshopped" photos and films, politicians telling outright lies, capitalist marketing, hyperrealism, the blurring of illusion and reality, had not been going on for some time. 9/11 and the Iraq War were events that were serious blows to any notion of national, public truth. Why is there a 9/11 Truth Movement, after all? Most of its key members are architects, engineers, professors, and scientists. The TV program *The X-Files* used the clever phrase, *The truth is out there*. But out where? Intellectually, the Postmodernist thinkers had pretty much completed the deconstruction of the notion of truth begun in the late 19th Century by Nietzsche. Nietzsche advocated for perspectivism…it all depends on your perspective, ranging from everyday superficial to the philosophically profound. Consider Paul Riceour's book *The Conflict of Interpretations*.

Someday I would like to write an essay on the smell of Postmodernism. But perhaps the smell of the death of "God" would get to me and be too much for me to complete it. But I offer this extended poem:

Our Postmodern Cauldron

What manner of world is this
we contemporaries have been fated to live our days in?
Where are we in the Time Spirit?
How many even have a clue?
How many realize what we are facing?

How many turn away from the signs
that are there for all to see?

Oh, hear then
the words of the poet who speaks of it—
Do you wish to know what the poet sees?
Hear then the words of the poet visionary—
The poet visionary has eyes open
& is not afraid to speak—

A Voice came to him—
It was the Voice of Psyche,
who said,
Tell it as you see it, poet.

The poet I am speaks,
as Psyche insists that I speak:

We live in a global,
madly pluralistic, Postmodern time,
a time of our World Fabric in chaos,
a transition time between Ages
we contemporaries have been fated to live in—
All around us, so close to us, palpable even,
is uncertainty, confusion, turmoil, anxiety,
our metaphysical disorientation for those who understand,
a silent unease is felt in the soul that cries out for answers—
But there are no answers in the Postmodern,
only old answers bankrupt no longer
inspiring us as living Mythos.

Everything & anything,
all Traditions in this cauldron of Postmodern,
are mashed together, a roiling mass without coherent Form,
a decadent culture is ours absorbing all,
accommodating all, but disempowering what it will...

all can be co-opted overnight by a System ravenous,
    with no soul.
Traditions
—our religions—despite millions who still
believe in them, are defunct, empty of the true
living Divine that once could speak to us,
no longer are they the living Mythos of Spirit—
Religions, exhausted, have unwittingly
abandoned & forgotten what is soul,
soul now having become only an abstract, lip-service word…
It is television though, movies, mass media,
the Internet, entertainment, social media mania…
    a multi-thousandfold smorgasbord
the populace is daily distracted by, to find itself
lost in, to be numbed by, to no longer see
anything of the glorious sky—
And across the news,
tensions are ongoing between competing,
faceoff nations, polarizations of threat,
senseless conflicts, constant little wars,
a psycho leader of Russia now invades Ukraine,
forcing such unconscionable, mindless daily
killing & suffering upon its people…
Armageddon a biblical prophecy,
constant rumors of World War III,
a nuclear doomsday clock is 90 seconds ever closer
    & closer to midnight,
the accepted insane global policy
we live with they call

MAD—

Mutual Assured Destruction,

would be the annihilation of us all, all of civilization,
our potential human finality, our very own extinction,

is every day in the balance, the nightmare lurking every night
    as we sleep…
Our nuclear global leaders, our military leaders,
bluntly put are sociopaths who play a most dangerous
chessboard game of power & dominance,
of existential threat that claims all who live
& breathe…

And American psychopath
crazed individuals make headline news
of weekly mass shootings, of shootings
in our schools—Why? Why?
our communities keep asking,
politicians talk each time of outrage,
consoling families, but futile are these words
that do nothing to prevent the next…
with murders taking place on everyday city streets,
police even liable for senseless killings…
In major cities, in capitals, protests of thousands
will march, unrest turned riots, we look
at the mayhem done in torn up downtowns—
And all wish & pray there must be an end
to this violence & killing, but politicians
have not a clue, and society moves on to the next
    Big Thing…
celebrities, sports & movie stars, pop star singers,
the Rich & the Famous, are always the favorites,
people seem to hardly get enough it seems,
transfixed by the sheer decadence of gossip fame & glitz.

Nihilistic materialism
our cosmic meaningless disorientation,
our science, our philosophy, our education,
presents no Greater Reality narrative but facts,
analysis, information—it's information overload anymore—,

it's all now digital social media just bouncing off
an image of one another…but where is soul?
In fact, life is really all about money, marketing,
business, profits, the Stock Market addiction,
it's the bottom line of the American mainstream—
Every day the mad lust for money, for power…
a society that worships Gods Moolah & Pow-ER.
Make money, make more money, to always want
more money, millionaires who want more money,
     billionaires not even satisfied…
Yes, own that big house, buy up more houses,
buy up properties, buy up cars, yachts, private planes…
Be a success, the 1980s heyday pressure was to be a success.
Everyone childhood conditioned to buy buy buy,
be the good consumer & keep buying—
Companies, corporations, expect greater profits,
yes, the bottom line *is* always profit, keep it coming…
TV commercials, radio commercials, magazine ads, all tell
     the story…

And scientists are mad
in bio labs…bioweapons, gain-of-function
virus insanity, a questionable pandemic
for a forced upon us New Normal,
or say, the Great Reset we hear
the World Economic Forum conspires…
Conspiracy agendas hide below the mainstream
in a Deep State, with a global elite, who still want more
     control—
Global elites want populations under their control,
& hints of a depopulation agenda for eventual global control,
Technos the new Superpower over all nations
& every day its increasing impact of AI
that would finalize control—
Already AI touted as civilization's

greatest danger…
or is it civilization's destined
new God?

And corporate
media giants toe the line, censorship
we find of different points of view, of freedom to think
    alternative views…
Technos has a Plan of a New World Order,
while Transhumanists want a new cyborg human,
mere biological humans they consider no longer
good enough for our planet—
They push
for more Technos, they push for AI,
they envision a coming fulfillment of the Plan.

As we find a warming planet
the climate scientists tell us,
anymore is common extreme weather,
droughts, fires, floods, storms of destruction,
Arctic & Antarctic, global glaciers, are melting,
every summer heat breaking records,
& still no preparation undertaken for our young generations,
it's projected as still all off in some future,
whatever the preferred Plan of Technos may come.
200 species every day are said to be dying,
that is to say, going extinct,
the 6th great mass extinction is underway
& populations remain unaware of the extent of what
    that means—
Human extinction unfortunately
is considered part of what this means…

But have no worry
with selfies, narcissism takes your mind off
all these worldly crises & all its madness & suffering—

Our culture cultivates Ego obsession,
Ego intoxication—just watch TV & see,
all manner of Ego incestuous behaviors
are there for all to see...
Yet therapists
are overwhelmed...client addictions,
anxiety, mental disorders, dysfunctional
relationships, depression, suicides quietly kept behind
    the news.
While Middle East Islam also worships the goods
of Technos, it remains Postmodern schizoid stuck
    in the Middle Ages...
repression the norm, ruthless suppression of women,
suppression of free expression, their punishments
given out that are utterly Medieval inhuman...

And in our skies,
ongoing UFO visitations, otherworldly
Watchers, for decades on, thousands
having seen them, yet coverups continue,
government & military still will not come
forward & disclose Other Intelligence is here
    across the skies of Earth,
the public rather must be kept strictly within
the conditioned human bubble...otherwise
admission of the truth of the UFO would shatter
the Postmodern Illusion that we are alone,
would shake society to its foundations
& open to us a multidimensional Universe.
But no Grand Narrative of cosmic Intelligences
our scientists are ready to tell, are even
prepared to tell, are even capable of telling.

And in the midst
of this Postmodern cauldron

of chaos, confusion, pluralistic decadence,
nihilism & madness, of spiritual disorientation,
is our transition between Ages—
We are entering a new Aquarian Age,
inevitably a New Story, a new Grand Narrative
that visionary Mythos-makers will tell,
a new orientation guided by our Higher Self,
in relationship to Other Intelligences,
acknowledging a new Revelation
of our cosmic Interconnectedness—
I am one among other visionaries
who hold this New Age Vision
revealed to me by Psyche,
to break us out, transform us out,
of this Postmodern cauldron.

February 2023

* * *

There was a once upon a time when thinking and traditional faith could co-exist. Traditional faith—that is, faith as belief, which is to believe doctrines passed down at secondhand, the dogmas of faith passed down—we find no longer acceptable because of the very nature of it having brought us ironically into a Postmodern world of disorientation and nihilism. Despite what billions on the planet might still believe, traditional religions can no longer sustain us. Carl Jung had already said back in the mid-20th Century that the Christ archetype, for example, of the Piscean Age no longer satisfied the emerging situation of our soul. This observation is now to be understood as referring to all world religions. The old Father "God" is dead and has been deconstructed, but that is not the end of the Story regarding Spirit and New Divinity. A New Story is beginning to unfold.

Reality as we know it is considered an utterly *Human* Reality. The thinkers and philosophy of recent centuries has clarified this for us, from Kant, Hegel, Marx, Freud, Nietzsche, Heidegger, Sartre, the analytical / language philosophers, the Postmodernists. This does not imply whatsoever, though, that Human Reality is predefined, limited, utterly self-referential, and already foreclosed on its potential. Human Reality is ever expanding, not only horizontally on the scale of our social, cultural, political, pragmatic intersubjectivity within world, but also vertically, on the scale of awakening consciousness, of the spiritual.

The great Hegel—there is much to learn from him as we go back to him, but at the same time we were fooled by him, we should have known better, as we realize he was no metaphysician who defied Kant—metaphysics being referenced here in the strong sense of an outside to Human Reality—but was the epitome of Logos mapping out the entirety of the human bubble. Spirit, (*The Phenomenology of Spirit*) developed in the mind of Hegel as becoming Absolute Knowledge, Absolute Spirit, was attained by the Concept (Logos, of course) *within* Human Reality. There was no Greater Reality of "God," or Other Intelligence outside of Human Reality; Hegel's own mind, he indirectly claimed, attained Godhood via strictly conceptual thought. Hegel saw his philosophy as the culmination, the end of, history. How pretentious does this sound to our ears today. (Similar to Francis Fukuyama today [his book *The End of History and the Last Man*] claiming that Neo-liberal Capitalism is now the culmination, the end, of history.) The bottom line is that Hegel's whole System was anthropocentric. Any outside to Human Reality was simply nonexistent, which is how he got around Kant and Kant's notion of noumena (an outside to Human Reality that we cannot know. In Hegel's philosophical System we can know all. No wonder Being was the empty universal and required to be filled in, made determinant, by conceptual Logos. *The Phenomenology of Spirit* (Spirit as Logos) completely elevated all phenomena within Human Reality to Absolute Knowledge. And our phenomenology today? I see Spirit as That-which-is-greater-than-us-coming-to-us, the active showing-to-us of Being. We are breaking out of anthropocentrism.

With Heidegger we also saw a loss of the sacred / spiritual dimension: in *Being and Time* there is no explicitly divine dimension to Dasein (human existence). For Heidegger, there is Dasein (German for existence, *our* human existence) and Being: Dasein facing Being alone and Being once again thought of in an anthropocentric way, despite Heidegger's valiant effort to try to get around any metaphysics that was only a revolving door of anthropocentric Human Reality. He used the strong word of "destroying" (Derrida would say "deconstructing") all past metaphysics. Yet, we must proceed with caution here…very few know the work of the later Heidegger and his halting attempt at thinking Mythos.

We know that in *Being and Time* Heidegger's original intention was to come to a new understanding of Being by a phenomenological understanding of our existence. Rather than being able to accomplish that, he provided an analytic of human existence (German 'Dasein'), with existential analyses of conformity (the they-self), care (our life is one of care for self), dread, anxiety, being-toward-death. But where in his analytic is love, joy, ecstasy, passion, the mystical, creativity, friendship? If we are to see *Being and Time* as primarily a study of human existence, rather than an attempt at thinking out thoroughly the question of Being (which he attempted in a stuttering way in his later work), we must note this shortcoming; in other words, it is surely incomplete. And Heidegger never did complete an intended Part 2 for *Being and Time*.

We can look at a poet during this same time period—Robinson Jeffers. Jeffers, too, exhibits this same poverty of Spirit…his experience of "God" is primarily through the abstract…yes, primarily celebrating the Beauty of things, of Nature above all. I do admire the poetry and long narrative poems of Jeffers, but once again, no Mythos. In neither of their cases—and in so many other writers and thinkers in the 20th Century—is there the richness of Spirit that a study of occult / esoteric metaphysics would reveal?

There was no covenant with Divinity. Of course a covenant with Divinity today would involve a new relationship to our own Higher/Divine Self, coming-to-us (in my Vision) as Divine Psyche. We might even imagine a covenant with an Other Intelligence if that Other Intelligence were genuinely intent on our further evolution.

Nihilism [Nietzsche]: That what were traditionally the highest values have lost their efficacy…there is no longer a transcendent basis to life…the transcendent has been emptied out of its traditional meanings. Nietzsche would not consider himself a nihilist, but his thinking insistently pointed out that our Traditions had brought about nihilism. The old gifts of Being are no longer effective, while Being itself is no longer experienced, and for a long time [Heidegger]. (Nietzsche primarily saw Being as a creative process Becoming.) Being shows a face of Nothingness to our world when considered nihilistically. [Consider Sartre's *Being and Nothingness*] Now Nothingness— the Void—is but one mask of Being. That Heidegger knew.

Existential crisis opens us to the mystery of Being. But we must be open…that is, philosophically to find ourselves in the Opening of Being, meaning that Being does open out to us an Opening to encounter "It," but, again, we must in some way be open for it. Today that implies that many of us now stand at The Edge of the collective existential crisis we are facing in order to develop a new encounter with Being. That new encounter comes-to-us via Spirit.

Is it possible that something from beyond The Edge of the world is coming-to-us? This coming-to-us from beyond The Edge of the world we will call in the most general sense Spirit, but Spirit as a new collective dispensation. (This is in contrast to personal spiritual experiences per se, as spiritual experiences are always happening for someone somewhere.) Spirit, from an existential-phenomenological stance, is always this coming-to-us. Spirit is this process of That-which-is-greater-than-us-coming-to-us. Greater-than-us refers to that which is greater than our everyday Ego-self reality. But now let us expand on that definition: That-which-is-greater-than-us-coming-to-us-revealing-Intelligence. For Spirit in its coming-to-us is not simply a nothingness, and not simply nonsense, not simply gibberish. A higher Intelligence is being revealed. Millions will still want to call that Intelligence "God." But that higher Intelligence happens to be of our own Higher/Divine Self.

For something to come-to-us, there must be a clearing, an opening, for it to come through. That is to say, it must be able to come-to-us through the transcendental horizon of a possibility. This is another way of referring to consciousness. That-which-is-coming-through is both a possible revealing Intelligence and the Opening itself of its own possibility. Of course we would have to speak here of a *higher* consciousness. And this we will also call the possibility of *novelty*. This is the supreme work of Spirit—Spirit as a supremely creative *process*.

There is a Call. We can consider it from different perspectives. It is the Inner Voice—the Call to our Self (capital S, in the Jungian sense). It is the Call to our Higher / Divine Self. It is the Call of new Divinity, Divine Psyche. It is the Call initiated by Spirit. It is the Call, the silent voice, of Being…but Being not as an empty abstract, but Being revealing the new Revelation, the new dispensation of the Ages—again, our own Divine Self, new Divinity coming-into the world. It is also the Call of the Age, the Zeitgeist, going out to all who can hear it. The Call cannot be denied or forgotten by those who hear it. The Call is "there," an ever presence, haunting us, always summoning us. Now it could be explained from other psychological interpretations… but do they inspire us into Mythos? That the Call inspires us to tell the New Story? To live, to find our Path as, the New Story?

An essential, traditional Christian notion that I have no interest in, that has no attraction for me, is salvation. The need for salvation has always seemed a cop-out to me, an existential flaw. The whole notion is a stale leftover from the ancient world. The Afterlife? Really now, how many today take some abstract Afterlife as more important than this life? When Christ comes to me, my question is not, *Will you save me?* but, *What can you teach me?*

Jesus died for our sins, says Christian doctrine. Oh really? What sins? What sins are we talking about? Something about that doesn't make sense. There's nothing I did that I can think of to justify Jesus dying on a cross for me. Is it that just being myself is sinful? Oh, Christian doctrine says it's the sin of being born human. So being born a human being is a sin? I wonder how many would agree with that. I certainly don't. This is definitely all part of an outdated Mythos.

So, do you want an instant breakfast religion? Just say, *Jesus Christ is my Lord and Savior*. That's it, that's all you need to say and you're ready to start your day. Ready to go out and make money and buy up all the things your little heart desires and consume everything in sight and get ahead of the pack—because Jesus has already saved you at breakfast.

Christians, you say you have a soul, but I say to you, You don't even know what soul is yet. Carl Jung pined that he had failed at what he saw as his most important life work—that of bringing into the world a solid understanding of the reality of soul, which is the reality of our psyche.

What is almost completely absent from everyday conversation, wherever we go, is reference to "soul." We are aware that the word has no use in a Postmodern society. Now I am not referencing the puff of mere abstraction that Christianity helped turn it into. Our conditioning has developed to always speak from Ego, and not let on that there is anything other than Ego (the Ego-self complex as depth psychology speaks of it...oh my, how people have even forgotten Freud). An alternative word is of course 'psyche.' But even the use of "psyche" is absent from everyday life. Again, the emphasis in this culture is on Ego-self, the Ego personality, as the center of Human Reality, the measure of all things...

What a society thinks of its poets is what society thinks of the soul. Poets have become the marginalized street persons of the culture. It is no surprise that soul in Postmodern life is a non-issue, an empty word, a ghostly anachronism from the past. In mainstream culture, the dominant culture, soul is never referenced, appears not to be a reality; if the word 'soul' is used at all, it is meant as a figure of speech. We must keep in mind that soul is another way of referencing our psyche.

Every day to be surrounded by people who have no self-conscious awareness of their own psyche. We might think, how is that possible? Our primary reality is psyche, and yet, most everyone thinks only of Ego. Everything is related to Ego...to Me, Me, Me. To Me, Myself, my self-image. When people say "I" do this, "I" do that, "I" am going there, do they ever think that their psyche would also be implied? But we live in a culture that does not foster awareness of our own psyche, of our own soul. The mainstream, mass media, the marketplace, consumerism, politics, entertainment, the tech world, are all focused on Ego. Getting ahead, making money, climbing the corporate ladder, be a success, get noticed, be a public figure, be a Somebody, are all driven by Ego. Even everyday idle chitchat rarely brings forth—mentions—self-awareness of psyche. And yet psyche is our primary reality...our life of feelings, emotions, moods, sensitivities, insights, imagination, fantasies, dreams, inspirations, creativity, our nightly dream world, our memories, our dark depths, our psychic potential, our Inner Voice, our Visions, our meditative thoughts for being open and listening, our metaphysical sense of a Larger Reality, our vastly greater life than our Ego-self projecting a persona, all is that of our psyche...that of our soul. Yes, people can talk about some of this, but do they ever imply their psyche, their soul?

Once again, to be surrounded every day by people who have no idea what the psyche is. Now isn't psychology a subject of study in colleges and universities? Do they ever teach that psychology is derived from the word 'psyche'? How many go to psychotherapy and still don't know what the psyche is? And here I am, a visionary, speaking of Divine Psyche as our New Age Divinity: No wonder but scarcely a few are even aware of what I am talking about. To understand first what psyche is remains key; but our mainstream culture could care less. Our mainstream culture conditions people to think only Ego, only Me Me Me. The Seventies were known as the Me Decade after all when narcissism became the Big Thing. Christopher Lasch explored all this in *The Culture of Narcissism* [1979].

Now when it came to the academic study of behaviorism, the psyche was simply taken out (forget about even mentioning soul). The notion of having a psyche was not only irrelevant, the psyche wasn't even considered a valid reality at all, not one, that is, that could be observed, measured, tested, experimented upon. Behaviorism wanted facts about behavior, period. Observing a person's behavior and developing methods to predict, modify, condition, regulate, even control, behavior was the focus; that was valid science, in agreement with other materialistically based sciences. Behaviorism, which was chartered academia, therefore made psychology scientific. We found the same with philosophical positivism—the psyche went utterly missing. Positivism wanted philosophy to take after the sciences.

Now we should begin to make the profound connection between our having a psyche and new Divinity coming-to-us as *Psyche*. So we have a psyche (soul), suppressed and repressed for approximately 2,000 years (the Christian/Islamic Piscean Age). Back in the 20th Century we had Freud,

Jung, Hillman, and various depth psychologists, dedicating their life work to bringing psyche back into the culture. The thing is, we still have a long way to go, what with Human Unevolved Darkness still dominating our soulful depths. Wouldn't it make in a destiny sense that sooner or later a visionary poet would come along who receives the Vision of Divine Psyche, our new Divinity, who would bring transformative Light into our Darkness and reveal the unlimited potential of our soul? Psyche, coming-to-us via Spirit, to enlighten us about our psyche. Makes perfect spiritual sense. Much of what I am hinting at here is further elaborated as we continue…

* * *

We need to spell out more this transition period between Ages we are currently living in that we have been calling the Postmodern; what, in other words, were the major characteristics of the Piscean Age that has been fading and those of the new Aquarian Age we are entering. Keep in mind that World Ages are approximately 2,160 years long, conveniently rounded off to 2,000 years.

Who would have thought that the fading Piscean Age—an Age attuned to the greater Universal (always implying "God") via belief, that is, oriented to dogmatic religion—would result in an utterly technological world? (Even history books will refer to the earlier half of the Piscean Age as an Age of Belief.) Now each astrological Age is actually defined by a polarity—the sign naming it that is its primary signature, but also the sign opposite it in the zodiac is an undercurrent theme that comes to beginning expression approximately halfway through the Age. The astrological undercurrent theme to Pisces is the sign Virgo—mind oriented to the material plane; the practical, rational, but also analytical, technically intellectualizing mind. (To prevent any misunderstanding, we are not referring here at all to personal astrology charts, but to World Ages). Halfway through the Piscean Age saw the Renaissance and the birth of modern science. Modern science and technology are perfect expressions of collective Virgo. So what about the new Aquarian Age then? The most obvious observation is that technology is taken to another level—invisible, instantaneous, long-distance, collective communication…and the best example is none other than the Internet. And the undercurrent theme to Aquarius—Leo, the sign expressly of creativity. And there are those of us who have already discovered that undercurrent energy—the Fountain of Unlimited Creativity.

Let us be quite aware, it is a very different world today—I'm especially thinking culturally—with the ubiquitous Internet. And the Internet, of course, is one of the Aquarian gifts of Technos; it is *Welcome to the Aquarian New Age*. Just about everyone is active on the Internet in one way or another. To imagine that thinkers, scholars, poets, writers, artists, over 30 years ago didn't have the Internet…and then let us consider those who lived further and further back. The Internet has become a universal cultural presence, implying a constant temptation, a constant always possible distraction, especially with social media, YouTube videos, podcasts. Years back, those involved with culture were not subject to the Internet's time-consuming temptations and distractions, they could simply pursue their work and find their audience in any number of traditional ways. Today, one is expected to have a presence on the Internet, via a website, email, social media, podcasts, blogs, YouTube videos, etc. Without some presence on the Internet, one's work today would probably have a difficult, if not a prolonged delayed time finding a wide audience; one's cultural presence would likely be nil. Even a guru, a spiritual teacher, who may never personally need to be on the Internet will undoubtedly have followers who will create an Internet presence for him to get his spiritual gifts and teachings out to the world. And that hints of the reality here—the Internet can connect us in ways, reaching out on a global scale, that were not previously possible.

How many of those in the past, if they could see us now, would frown and scoff at the millions of us "addicted" to the Internet. For all of my own critical perspective on Technos, would I ever think to abandon the Internet? But, again, we have to fully realize, it is an utterly different world today, an utterly different cultural milieu; to be or not be active on the Internet, especially for 100% of the young, is no longer considered just an option…accessing the Internet in the New Age has become a given. Curiously, this happens to be very unlike television—one can easily choose not to watch or even have a television (I don't), no matter how common it is assumed watching television is.

What is the further implication of Aquarius? If the new, alternative symbol for Aquarius (alternative to the traditional Water Bearer), is, as I claim, The Fountain, what is it about fountains? Fountains are like geysers, pouring forth water that was first hidden from view up into the air. The Fountain of Aquarius—The Fountain of Illumination—pours forth all that has been hidden in the dark Waters of the previous Age (Pisces a Water sign) into the open Air (Aquarius an Air sign) for all to see, into the open Air of open-minded, free communication. And what has been hidden in the dark Waters? All that remains hidden in the Unconscious, all that has been repressed, suppressed, covered up, for 2,000 years…and today that includes all the propaganda lies, conspiracies, the machinations of the power elites. Also all the hidden wisdom of the past, all its hidden secrets, which is exactly what is meant by the word 'occult.'

This is why some pursue conspiracy research: That the secret power brokers—the power elite—hold secrets, conspire behind closed doors, automatically raises our suspicions at this point in our history, or, better yet, in our psychospiritual evolution. Yes, someone is bound to say, Well, there have always been conspiracies, what's the big deal? Well, yes, in the past that was the case. But, sorry, it is a big deal anymore. If we keep in mind that we are moving out of the Piscean Age, when holding secrets and conspiracy agendas was a given, then we begin to understand why this move towards greater openness and transparency grows in importance. As we move squarely into the Aquarian Age, holding secrets and conspiring behind the scenes will no longer be acceptable. The Aquarian intention is to bring out what was hidden into the open for all to see. Of course this has radical implications for society, as indeed it should.

We are leaving behind the Piscean Age when things could be kept hidden, secret, in the dark, suppressed, repressed. Think of all the secrets kept by governments. Think of all the cover-ups. In the new Aquarian Age we have been entering, secrets will be more difficult to keep hidden, as all that is hidden is potentially to be revealed. In other words, transparency will be promoted. This is one implication of the new spirituality. Those who think only in terms of their own personal spiritual advancement—I want enlightenment for myself—are still back in the Piscean Age. The Aquarian Age calls for a collective spirituality of openness, as we will eventually access the Internet of the Mind Field.

Aquarius: an Air sign, and as with all Air signs, it signals some kind of mental activity, especially involving communication. Aquarius is also a fixed Air sign. I interpret that, in one sense at least, that we will no longer be satisfied with only abstract mind—mouthing metaphysical abstractions, for example—but will work on bringing mind into greater concreteness. Instead of, say, Spirit or Higher Self as nice ideas to give lip service to, we want to experience them more specifically, more concretely, to spell out more thoroughly what they are about. Instead of saying, Yes, we have a psyche, it is to actually know firsthand all the complex details of our psyche, which is why Psyche will be the Divine Teacher of all the labyrinthine corridors of our psyche.

We need to spell out a bit more the new Aquarian spirituality, what I call a Divine Psyche spirituality. Aquarius is an Air sign, so the energetic attunement will be of the mind, the mental—but especially of the higher mind, which is shorthand for our Ego-self developing a relationship with Higher Self, our Divine Self experienced as Divine Psyche. Air is the element of thinking, language, and most importantly, communication. Air is the open mind, freed of constraints, impositions, limitations, doctrines, dogmas…eventually freed of its mass-minded conditioning—the herd mind. But as a fixed sign Aquarius, yes, can imply a mental propensity for fixity on opinions, ideas, positions, causes. I prefer to see it as a moving away from the abstract to the mentally concrete. At the same time, Aquarius is Air of the higher mind, a knowing for oneself firsthand—*gnosis*. It is to develop first of all the universal psychic ability of intuition. Ultimately, it is the Call to develop the ability to enter the invisible Mind Field consciously, concretely. Aquarian spirituality is therefore not the spirituality of passive surrender and secondhand belief, which was the attunement of the previous Age of Pisces.

An Aquarian spirituality of Psyche takes the reality of the psyche seriously. It implies that our psyche develops its concreteness with guidance from Psyche (from one of Psyche's multifaceted guises). This is not an Eastern spirituality that many Westerners took as a yearning for transcendence (which was strong in the 1980s), for getting rid of the Ego, for getting spiritually "high," for an enlightenment that is more suitable for living in a monastery. This is bringing Spirit coming-to-us today as Psyche into the concreteness of our psyche, by making our psyche explicit in all our experience. It is the embodiment of "Know Thyself"—but, again, not a know thyself as mere abstractness, such as Consciousness is All, Everything is One, I am the Universe, nirvana is return to Nothingness, I extinguish myself in mystical Oneness, and thereby thinking that by simply mouthing any of this we are thereby being spiritual. It is to know thyself as embodied in this world; it is to know thyself from our actual being-in-the-world.

So, then, what are some of the implications of this new Aquarian spirituality? Of making our psyche concrete? Here are some:

> Coming to know your Ego complex.
> Being able to interrogate and deconstruct your own Ego.
> Coming to know your life Path, its destiny, on a Mythos level.
> Being able to carry on inner dialogues, not just let fragments of dialogue chatter like mindless monkeys, but to actually have coherent dialogues with your Higher Self…perhaps to even be able to write them out or share them with another to get at the point of them.
> Being able to confront the Powers within us—to name them, to carry on dialogues with them.
> Being able to unravel the Threads that make up your existence. In our relationships, to unravel what is unspoken—finding a way to make the dynamics at play conscious.
> To be willing to take the journey into the darkness of soul, the Labyrinth of soul—to bring Light into your darkness.
> To develop intuition so that you can quickly see the essence of a situation or quickly untie a knot of intellect thought.
> Bringing what is inside of you out of you so that communication at a higher level can take place. And not just talk about it in the abstract, as so many popular cultural figures do— we already have plenty of books of tedious, long-winded, abstract talk. But how many are Mythos?

* * *

Especially years ago, I would meet New Agers or other spiritually oriented Eastern followers who wanted to rid themselves of their Ego, usually seeking, almost desperately, a way of transcending out of the Ego. Their attempts were always in vain. There is no eliminating of the Ego—it was, after all, the evolutionary trajectory of humanity to develop an Ego—but now there is the next stage of our evolution—the transformation of the Ego. And the process? By connecting with our Higher, our Divine, Self. Once in a relationship with Higher Self, Ego begins transforming out of its conditioning, out of its perceived limitations, out of its complexes and hangups, out of its narcissism...it accesses a greater, more universal, consciousness. It is then on its way toward becoming more akin to one's Higher Self. This is indeed the evolutionary intention, is it not?

All religious Traditions, esoteric schools, spiritual systems that claim to have the Truth, that claim to have it all mapped out for us already so that there is nothing especially creatively new for us to do, are actually for me signposts leading to dead ends that belong in the past. Why do I stay in a spiritually creative process? Because it means, there is no final Truth, no Absolute, to attain, no final Answer to everything, there is no final destination to get to, no Theory of Everything to go mad about, not even the great abstract Consciousness is All to get blissed out about. And I remain wary of seductive neon signs that say, *Here is Mastery*. Let us instead passionately pursue new Mythos, the New Story that will be never ending, never having to claim, Here is the final Truth. This is what our new encounter with Being implies.

The Unconscious is a vastly larger realm than our Ego self-consciousness; it is the hidden Darkness—Human Unevolved Darkness—always-here-with-us. Soul can be said to be the feeling and mood texture of our conscious experience (synonymous with our psyche) but is also largely hidden in the Darkness always-here-with-us. Soul, what Christianity had utterly repressed and slighted, I see as essentially our hidden potential...what is in fact ultimately an unlimited potential. First, it is our potential-to-be (our "everydayness" as the early Heidegger wrote of), but then, even more significantly, it is our potential-to-become (what Nietzsche always wanted to emphasize).

Our Human Unevolved Darkness—these are the labyrinthine corridors within the depths of our Unconscious. Our Darkness that almost all shrink from facing, that politicians and CEOs dare not speak about if they are even that aware. Our Darkness manifesting at times as anger, hate, bigotry, greed, violence and killing. Our Darkness manifesting as wars and military arsenals, as nuclear weapons, biological weapons…manifesting as global power contentions. It is Spirit coming-to-us that would bring its Light of new Divinity into every labyrinthine corridor of our unevolved Darkness, to transform our Darkness. Another implication of The Fountain of Illumination and The Fountain of Transformation—The Fountain that is the Living Symbol of the new Aquarian Age. The Fountain in which Psyche was revealed to me.

Our Human Unevolved Darkness—until that is seriously addressed in an open, public, global way, we will continue to have polarizing groups, political parties, factions, peoples, countries, at each other's throats, ready to promote hatred, initiate violence, start wars, bringing more suffering of peoples into the world. This would involve an in-depth process both psychological and spiritual—in other words, a psychospiritual process. Scarcely anyone in public life would even attempt this or would even know how to go about such a process. Their understanding of our psyche and its Darkness is nil; all they know is the Ego reality of money, power, and prestige. And here we are, here the world stands, ready to let Human Unevolved Darkness express hatred and start war after war. Even on a personal level this processing of psyche is uncommon. Is it any surprise that our new Divine Teacher would be the new Divinity of Psyche?

The contemporary approach to technological mastery requires a whole civilization; it is a collective project requiring multitudes of individuals and complex infrastructures. The spiritual approach to mastery traditionally but requires one individual person with a practice, one who is most often called an adept, an arhat, a guru, a Zen, or yogi master…yes, even an avatar. But a Mythos, which is really a collective Form? Ideally it requires a whole culture, if only initially a subculture, that is oriented to a Greater Reality.

We have this window called futurity—we can envision a possible future. When did this window of futurity come into play? The Greeks did not obsess about the future. Did any ancient peoples obsess about the future? It was Christianity…and the hope for a future life, in the Afterlife. But then in the late Middle Ages, into the Renaissance, in the early craft guilds, among the alchemists, emerged the notion of the perfectibility of humanity… Roger Bacon, Leonardo de Vinci, Francis Bacon, then Descartes, soon the early scientists… It was the birth of the religion of technology. [See David F. Noble, *The Religion of Technology*]

Today, we are in the creative position of consciously determining our future, which was the thrust of the work and writings, for one, of Barbara Marx Hubbard, in particular her books *Conscious Evolution: Awakening the Power of our Social Potential* and *Emergence: The Shift from Ego to Essence*. She hit the proverbial nail on the head. Or we think of R. Buckminster Fuller and his inspired work, lectures, and books, such as *Utopia or Oblivion* and *Operating Manual for Spaceship Earth*.

We have heard it said that our traditional spiritual responses have not kept up with our technological world. Now think about that—isn't this telling regarding our religious traditions. Doesn't a statement like that implicate first of all, above all, our religious traditions? That statement alone says that our traditions, as they stand, are inadequate in the face of a Postmodern world dominated by Technos. In terms of traditional Christianity, we could say to this, Well, hasn't "God"—hasn't Jesus, for that matter—had plenty of time to inspire us with new responses to our world? Isn't the silence of "God" telling? Radical theologian Thomas J.J. Altizer has much to say about that [*Radical Theology & the Death of God*]. (And to mention for a moment Neale Donald Walsh's series of books *Conversations with God*: Rather than "God," I would say he has been having conversations with Higher/Divine Self.) It would then be a New Age response that would fully address our contemporary world and would strive to be an adequate spiritual response to the new cybertechnologies that are moving us into the realm of Interconnectedness and the Invisible, unfortunately at this time without Spirit. New Age spirituality and the new cybertechnologies are indeed advancing on parallel tracks, are they not? Both are on the frontiers of Aquarius.

As has become quite apparent, there is no traditional religion that is capable of confronting Technos. That makes sense when all traditional religions were already established long ago, long before the world became a technological world. This is why we must talk about the transformation of all religions. I know, I know, so many will say, But we are not creative enough to do that! Really now, that's what I get from just about all of my contemporaries. But that is the super-creative challenge we face, is it not? Again, I can hear, You are asking us to engage in creativity at a level that is beyond us! beyond our capabilities! beyond what we can even envision! Why, yes, indeed, as a New Age herald, that is exactly what I am asking for...

Of course we can study the religious Traditions and learn much, about life, the possible meaning of life, about what our life Path might be, about higher levels of consciousness, about the (esoteric) metaphysics of a Greater Reality. One could study the Traditions or even one Tradition for years. One could be content with following a particular Tradition, and millions of people are. But we have realized that our Traditions as a whole are inadequate in our greater Postmodern techno-materialistic world. So we realize that the transformation of the Traditions is called for. That is one aspect of the Call of the Age. But what, then, is the key here? Or let us put it this way: How would one go about transforming our Traditions without first receiving a Vision, a Revelation? Without an original Vision, how would one even proceed in this process? A Vision can initiate the process of transforming; it offers the gnosis of seeing into a possible future and creatively knowing how to engage the Traditions so that a new global picture can unfold. A Vision, a Revelation, requires then the art of Mythos...Mythos-making that might indeed bring a new global picture into the world. An extremely challenging destiny indeed.

If we are serious about pursuing an enlightened New Age, then past organized belief—religions—are no longer our foundation. We are no longer simply "believers" in what has been passed down to us as secondhand doctrine, dogma, or teachings. It is one thing to study old religions, to learn something of their teachings, as part of our universal education, but then, not to simply believe in them at face value as our life foundation. Belief per se was an existential attunement of the Piscean Age; the new Aquarian Age is one of gnosis—a knowing for oneself firsthand of spiritual and metaphysical matters. I know for myself because I have been shown directly by Spirit and I have seen. This is the initial step in a Mythos that is living. Yes, the Aquarian New Age can be considered a rebirth of Gnosticism…but, again, not simply accepting at face value any particular ancient teachings of the Gnostics, but experiencing, realizing, gnosis for oneself. Need it be said, this is also a revaluation of creativity in the most profound sense. It is to say, I have entered The Fountain of Illumination and know firsthand of its Unlimited Potential.

I say,
> *Believe little.*
> *The most important thing is,*
> *experience for yourself firsthand.*

Know that the Aquarian motto is,
> *Experience firsthand—*
And where experience leaves you
with questions rather than quick answers,
I say,
> *Remain open.*

It is said, But people need to believe in something greater, something of universal, transcendent significance, than our everyday Human Reality… there must be something more to life than work, sex, entertainment, raising families, and eventual death. Religion—usually meaning religions from the past, the ancient past—has historically been the Answer that people need. Religions help people cope with the uncertainties and questions of life. Yes, indeed, but religions of the past are no longer adequate in a New Age world. So…a New Age religion? Any potential New Age religion will not look the same as religions of the past. That would ignore the meaning of a New Age. Once again, it would be founded on gnosis and be co-created by collaborating individuals into Form as a living Mythos.

It is apparent today that there are those of us who form an invisible network of awareness. Globally, there must be millions of us by now. What primarily defines us is that we are not in enthrallment to mainstream media, and we do not uncritically accept the mainstream, official, government narrative on events. We are not willing to be naïve. We are aware that there is a bigger picture to global events, that elite powers have a long-term agenda that is obviously in their favor, that there is more going on behind the scenes than officialdom would want us to know. (Think about the UFO coverup.) And we are not to be lulled into laziness about going no further with what we assume already, as we are diligently doing our research homework of becoming more and more aware. We are largely invisible—there is likely no one organization that we belong to. Though we do not necessarily agree with one another on all the details of our findings, or use the same language for expressing it, we constantly share our insights with one another. We, hopefully among the majority of us, are acting on our awareness in constructive ways that expose the threats that we see. Even more, that we are working to advance an alternative Vision to what the mainstream offers up on the news. Others we know may not share this awareness with us for one reason or another, whether family or friends. Yes, even friends we might have known for years may prefer to remain in the dark about us belonging to this network. In the broadest sense, so that this does not just hang in mere abstractness, we are all part of an evolving awareness network that is ever vigilant of the threat of a growing elite-driven AI future that has all the appearance of plotting total control of all life on Earth.

I know that this is a hard realization for many to swallow: That traditional religions, as they stand, are at an evolutionary dead-end. A New Age, and a new spirituality, even if it transforms into a religion, bringing all traditional religions into this co-creative process, implies that its New Story is an evolutionary advancement for humanity.

There are those who assume that already some thousands of years ago the Eastern sages have done all of our spiritual work for us. Sit at the feet of a guru or yogi master, or seriously read the Vedas, the Upanishads, or the Bhagavad Gita, and you will find all that you need. As if what the Eastern sages have

103

mapped out regarding the various stages/levels of consciousness had been set for all time. As if the human spirit has exhausted its creative potential—and I mean specifically psychospiritually, not scientifically, technologically.

We hear from those who are theologically oriented that people need some form of transcendence in their life to make their life truly meaningful. That is of course where religions came in. But traditional religions are helpless to address a world that is completely in the clutches of the God Technos. Does the New Age have an answer regarding transcendence? Yes, it is connecting with our own Higher/Divine Self…that we humans have a divine dimension to ourselves. This is what Heidegger missed, what Sartre missed, what all the positivist and analytical and Postmodern philosophers who had dominated the mental milieu of the 20th Century missed. But, no, it wasn't simply an oversight. All their thinking, which was anti-metaphysical (metaphysical in the philosophically academic sense), denied any such thing as our having a divine dimension. That is why so much of their thinking only leads to dead ends (oh, perhaps, yes, only to further hyper-intellectualizing). Now, Higher Self…do not assume that Higher Self is not transcendent enough, as if we already know the full reality of our Higher/Divine Self. To be completely honest, we hardly know much. Oh, but someone will undoubtedly stand up and say, Eastern religions do have all the answers for that. Eastern religions are traditional religions, helpless as are all traditional religions, to confront and challenge a technological world. Again, our major concern here is not that individuals cannot find answers for themselves personally in traditional religions, but that we here have taken on the role of visionary thinkers addressing the collective, our current global Postmodern societies. Yes, individuals can find their life Path, but what Form of newly emergent transcendence can face off and confront Technos?

When we refer to our Higher Self, this is definitely not the possible misconception of thinking that we are simply trying to inflate our Ego-self to be some "God." We are referring to the various higher levels of consciousness beyond the Ego-self, to a collective Mind Field of the astral-psychic, to the Archetype of all Humanity, to our Christ-self, to our higher relationship with Spirit, to an Interconnectedness with all that Being reveals

104

to us that has no limit. To the Ego, all of this is certainly transpersonal… yes, transcendent, let us say. It is all literally overwhelming to the Ego. And to develop a relationship with our Higher Self? First is having at least some experience that revealed to us a Higher Self. Hinduism knows full well what all this implies in its own notion of Atman.

Okay, so I will hear—there was a whole women's movement behind this in the 1980s—, but it is Goddess who is coming back into our world. Well, that is Psyche. Or we hear of the return of Sophia…well, that is Psyche. Or it is Jesus who we should anticipate…well, that is Psyche. Or, it is Shakti/Shiva… well, that is Psyche. Or the supreme Hindu Atman…well, that is Psyche. Psyche has many names and can reveal many Forms. Wouldn't Divinity in the New Age reveal to us a multidimensional Form to teach us of our own unlimited potential?

It is especially Goddess, though, who pulls us back to the mythic—the mythic mode of our being, the mythic dimension that especially emerges out of our relationship with the natural world. Of course, I see this as *Mythos*. Whereas "God" pulls us toward the otherworldly, the abstract, disconnecting us from Earth, Goddess says, *Enough with your abstract theology! Enough with this vain yearning for an Afterlife! Enough with your clever language games! Enough with your tinsel flashing virtuoso intellect! Enough with your Ego manipulated metaphors! Enough with your secondhand myths of the past!* Those who open to Goddess (one of the guises of Divine Psyche) will know of some version of these divine injunctions firsthand. Goddess brings us back to gnosis, and the Mythos which is co-created from gnosis.

* * *

I tend to not take seriously, perhaps even to mistrust at times, anyone who has opinions and answers sticking out of their pocket, like a wad of cash for the Ego to use in any circumstance. Rather, when we realize that more in-depth conversation requires that we must consider the interconnectedness of the Web of Being, we find that we must pause, slow down, and think over what we want to say, and how to proceed. Perhaps in the moment we cannot say anything definitive. But we can remain open to the issue at hand…we will look into it, mull it over, and later share tentatively what our thoughts are.

How many even know how to mull things over anymore? How to chew on a thought, an idea, until it becomes a nutrient in a larger body of thought. How to ponder in the night when all the daily madness of the world settles down. It is considered awfully smart to be able to immediately spout off opinions and facts and name drop at the snap of the fingers. But to be able to pause in conversation with another and let the true complexity of thought take its own time to come through, how many are practiced at that?

Waiting, Being Open, Listening

Friend, I can't help but see how you keep rushing about.
Can you just pause for a moment?
Just pause for a moment and put yourself
in a place of waiting so that you can be aware.

Waiting? What's this waiting business?
Be aware of what?
Do you want to talk about something?

If you would just stop and pause, I will tell you.
Together we can pause and come to wait
and be aware, right here, right now.

But waiting for what?
I don't have time to wait around.
Sorry, but I have things to do,
so many things to do—
I have so much to do.

But can't you stop for just a bit?
I am asking if you can just wait
for Nothing for a change.
And while we wait for Nothing,
that you can be open—

Wait for nothing? Be open?
Be open to nothing?
What is this open business?
Do I have the time for such nonsense?
To wait and be open to nothing?

Well, how can you know what being open is
if you can't stop, pause, and wait a bit?

But what am I being open about?

I am asking you to be open to—

Open to—to what?
You are not making sense.

Perhaps a new sense—

What sense is that?

If you knew that already,
you wouldn't need to be open for it—
You would already have it now, wouldn't you?

I would already have what?
What is it that I am supposed to be open to?
Am I supposed to do something?

You don't have to do anything,
but in your awareness,
wait and be open and listen—

Listen? What am I listening for?

Listen for what comes to you.

I have thoughts about what
I am supposed to be doing.
Is something else supposed to come to me?

This all sounds like nonsense.

But this is the new sense—
That which will come to you
is approaching you in the silence.
I can tell you this, it is called Spirit.
And if you can wait, be open, and listen, Spirit will come.

Spirit? What is this spirit business?
I don't believe in such a thing.
I hear nothing but my constant thoughts.

But if you can wait a bit,
out of this Nothing, Spirit will come
to you and speak to you.
It might even overwhelm you.

This nothing? How can nothing do that?
This has really gotten to be too much.

Too much, you say?

This is too much for me right now.

Then you are here, in the right NOW.
You now experience the "too much."
Spirit is the too much.

You know, I am getting overwhelmed
by this whole conversation.

Good—this is Spirit, this is what Spirit does.
To be overwhelmed by too much
is exactly the impact that Spirit makes.

What is this spirit business?
This is really about nothing.

But this Nothing is showing you so much,

that it has apparently gotten to be too much, as you say.

No, this conversation is too much.

Good—Spirit has a way of coming into Language.

You mean, this crazy talk.
Like anything is nothing
and nothing is anything.

You will find that anything
and everything will be coming to you,
if you can stay in this place for a bit.
At least give it a try.

What place? A place of nothing?

A place of waiting, being open, and listening.
A place of Spirit coming-to-you and saying.

Saying? Saying what? What can nothing—
this spirit whatever—say to me?

It can say a lot, enough to be overwhelmed.

But I have a lot of things to do—
I have to go now—I must go—
I'm really feeling anxious about this.
I need to do things.

You're feeling anxious perhaps about the too much.

Yes, this is too much.
I need to go and do something.

Okay. Do whatever you have to do.
But for me? I have Nothing to do
right now, and in this Nothing to do,
Spirit shows me the too much,

and Spirit says, Here, Now, is BEING.
Yes, BEING, the too much, the overwhelming,
the overflowing, the perpetually showing,
the perpetually giving, the constantly up-rushing, joyous Fountain.

Ah, my friend, you didn't wait long enough
to experience the joy of how

EVERYTHING IS.

January 2021

* * *

We find that religion is often a way for otherwise non-metaphysical people to feel a waft of profundity blowing through their lives. They can feel the equal of any thinker simply because they believe in "God," who, of course, is the Absolute thinker, the Ultimate thinker, the Almighty Creator of the entire Universe, and because they believe they are on close terms with such a Supreme Being because they are indeed believers, they feel then that they are on the inside track of divine profundity. They therefore believe they possess the Truth, the ultimate Answer to life.

More and more I'm aware of those out there who are pursuing what they feel are cutting-edge, visionary projects, but are so often isolated individuals. Noble efforts they make, but they need to connect more with others; I know, I am in the same situation. In our current culture, everyone is assumed to be doing their "own thing," but the lone wolf approach doesn't appear to do much these days. Haven't the Hopi elders told us that this is no longer a time for the lone wolf? Look, there are those of us who are available to provide feedback, constructive advice, perspective, collaboration, especially given my own experience with Mythos. Again and again I see visionary efforts fail because individuals have no Mythos grounding...

Instead of encouraging us to think in terms of community, *our* community to start with, for decades now, the mainstream emphasis has been on the Ego-self. *It's all about YOU,* as the phrase went some years ago. Of course that meant properly adjusting to our consumer, capitalist System…getting a job, ideally a good job, making good money, getting ahead, making more money, increasing your savings account, becoming a success…and continue to buy up material things to your heart's delight…oh, and don't forget, obsessing about finding the right partner. This has been all about enhancing one's self-image, the Ego. And don't neglect to constantly pay attention to celebrities as they set the image of what the ideal person is. Look, just turn on your TV, it's all in plain sight…or listen to mainstream radio or peruse slick mainstream magazines. Mainstream conditioning is all pervasive. Despite this criticism, this in no way is to deny that individuals have their own life Path, that individuals have an inner soul Calling to develop their own individuality, which implies the whole psyche, not just Ego. We need to keep in mind, the Aquarian New Age motto is *Individuality within community*.

Looking Out for Number One [Robert Ringer] was the title of a book back in 1977. Yes, the title alone was a great promotion to Ego-centered individuals pursuing personal success involving relationships, career, money, etc. Was there any expressed concern for others, for community, or for the Earth?

The focus on self, to the degree of being obsessed with self, can be grossly Ego-centered, readily verging on narcissistic. What it lacks is another important theme of the new Aquarian Age, and that is *community*. The focus on Self—individuation, Jung would say—takes place in a context; that context, not to be simply abstract, ideally is at home and fostered in, and in turn fosters, a community. And how many today truly live in community with others? The dominant cultural mainstream has no genuine notion of it. Some small towns may have it. Or perhaps very defined spiritual communities where you must abide by their teachings and doctrines. And there are a few intentional communities out there. Self in community…that is, individuals, though perhaps rejecting the mainstream, in the Aquarian New Age will be called to pursue their Path in life in true community with others.

What we need to become more aware of as it is so ingrained in our contemporary world, in the everyday society we live in, is the unmitigated reality of competition. The degree of competition out in the Capitalist, consumer marketplace is not only obsessive, but also manic, a madness, a sickness, that is simply taken for granted. Competition in sports is one thing, belonging in sports, going back, in fact, to ancient Greece. But the competition we see in industry, in business, in marketing, in consumerism, has grown to such a degree that we could do without it. The same goes for politics. In politics, it appears to be tearing our country apart. Given that civilization may be nearing The Edge of a possible MELE, it is becoming of necessity that more cooperation among those with wealth and power is fostered. That companies and corporations might engage in cooperating with one another in order to address the crises we face—is that a joke? Is there even any understanding of that? What might that entail? What might that require of the human soul in our Ego-centered, Ego-obsessed, Ego-driven, world? The business Ego only wants more—more customers, more money, more wealth, more influence, more power over the market. This is under the rubric called neoliberalism, a totally cutthroat free market with no regulations and no social ethics. And we see what this ideology is doing to us…and it has become sick.

Many years ago I was naive to think that depth psychology, as primarily developed by Freud, Jung, and further developed by Hillman and a number of other Jungian/archetypal/depth psychologists, would somehow be the key in bringing enough psychological understanding into society that we would see a major shift in enlightened practice in all areas. Boy, was I off—I came to realize that the great majority has no interest in depth psychology, the power elites have no interest whatsoever in self-understanding, so the audience for depth psychology is extremely small and at the same time has been academically most often considered "fringe"…and so, once again, the dark, seething forces in incestuous human self-interest are untouched by ideas of the Ego, the Unconscious, of psyche, of complexes, archetypes, and updated interpretations of old myths. Depth psychology has so far gone nowhere in the transformation of society. I saw that something far more radical, a truly new Revelation, had to come into play.

Many years ago I was also naive to think that astrology could somehow be key in bringing psychological understanding into society so that individually and collectively we could work through our conflicting issues. Disappointingly, I came to realize that the great majority don't really take astrology that seriously, to begin with; for many, it is considered "occult," an anachronism from the past, and the academic world (which represents knowledge as endorsed by the dominant power establishment) considers it pseudo-knowledge (something akin to outdated mythology). You also find that even those who do know their chart don't necessarily take it all that seriously enough. So, once again, the dark, seething forces in incestuous human self-interest are essentially untouched by another symbolic system for self-understanding.

When we refer to the texture of Time, that a certain period of Time—the Zeitgeist—has a "feel" to it, that there is a collective tone to the Age, that the memory feel, for example, of 50 years ago, or 30 years ago, does not have the same feel as today, it can be easily passed off as merely subjective, it is only a personal thing referring to an individual's age, who is of course always getting older. When the emphasis is shifted to the individual like this, we lose the collective experience of Time, and the possibility of its Mythos. We utterly neglect that the texture of a Time period has an astrological basis to it.

What we will see emerging, in one form or another, is a new kind of hero. The Age has been calling for it. The image, the concept, of this hero is starting to be articulated out of the collective. We are rapidly realizing what we are up against today. Eyes have been opening. Ears have been opening.

The new kind of hero—it is not as if this is a clearly profiled figure in the mainstream so that it could readily become co-opted. This may be as much a Mythos figure as any actual person. Because we know today what we are up against. The work to be done must often go invisible, as well as be visible at points. This new kind of hero can also be considered the new warrior:

The New Warrior

You do not look to the past,
your model of warrior is not found in the past,
you do not aim to practice the old arts of aggression—
To you, killing others is an abomination.
Yes, warriors in the past were often heroes,

113

but I say, that is no longer the way of the hero—
The warrior today must be on a whole new Path,
an orientation not set into play by psychopathic
leaders, by power players & elites who need others
to play warrior for them to secure their dominance
      agendas…
What our civilization
is crying out for is a new kind of warrior—
A global change is called for, an Earth-loving
      transformation…
A new warrior is called for, has a Mission,
holds before himself/herself a Vision of this transformation,
the warrior today practicing truly new creative arts—
Starting with himself & herself…going into
the darkness of self, processing that darkness
—this is soul work that calls to be done—,
daring then to understand our differences,
having the courage to expose global elite agendas,
unafraid to speak out, to act in unusual, unexpected ways,
using arts psychospiritual, esoteric & energetic,
      arts that speak new Mythos—
Such a warrior promotes true global community,
      out of a love of humanity…

Such a warrior looks to the future—
That is what a Vision entails, what a Vision projects.
Such a warrior is no longer Ego aggressive,
a naïve pawn for power players, that *they*
can accomplish *their* will—
Such a warrior is savvy of worldly affairs,
yet has firsthand knowing of a Greater Reality.
Such a warrior is heart-felt sensitive to others,
determined to bring Spirit Universal to all.
Such a warrior may be unheralded,
but whose time is coming—

Listen.
There is a Calling
going out precisely for new warriors of futurity—
Are *you* such a warrior?

March 2023

* * *

Gods and Goddesses

Ancient peoples in all lands knew of Gods and Goddesses. Still today in India people worship in various ways different Gods—Vishnu, Shiva, Shakti, Brahmin, Atman, Kali, and that is only a few of the dozens of their other Gods. In the far distant ancient world, in Sumer and the various empires of Mesopotamia, in Egypt, the Gods once had such an overwhelming influence on us. They were superior, super-human; they were all powerful; they had superior knowledge, which is an understatement. The ancients were in awe of them. They worshipped them. The Gods were immortal. They dominated us, as we often were their servants, their slaves, we were their subjects. But at some point, they also became our teachers, teaching us the arts and skills of civilization. (Didn't Zecharia Sitchin have plenty to say about this in his various books?) The ancient Greeks had a pantheon of Gods—the major Olympians and various other Gods who oversaw so many everyday functions. The memory of them was absorbed into our Unconscious—Jung's Collective Unconscious, so that our psychology in the West was molded by their various powers. But in the Christian and then in the Modern Era, they were relegated to mere myth; humanity, it was said by scholars, had gone through a so-called ancient mythic phase. With our new UFO glasses, however, we now have a new understanding of who these Gods were—Other Intelligences active on Earth.

Might there be Gods who are powers for us today? Might Gods be acting through us, that is, through society, today? I am thinking here of worldly Gods who are primary Powers in our civilization today. We could say Gods are still present to us in our everyday world. It is Psyche who can interpret

115

these Powers for us and bring them into Mythos. The Inner Voice of Psyche can help us discern their voices in the various areas of our life. It is Mythos that can bring them into Form. Is Logos capable of this? No, scientific, Ego-centered Logos would say this is all just fantasy.

Our soul is naturally polytheistic. Depth psychology has explicitly confirmed this; James Hillman wrote extensively of our soul having an affinity for various Gods and Goddesses, beginning with his ground-breaking book *Revisioning Psychology*. Setting depth psychology aside, though, our own life experiences should have hinted at this to begin with. Which is why Christianity had to repress the soul and suppress all forms of polytheism in its 2,000-year dominance. It was the Ego that required monotheism. The emergence of the Ego and the birth of monotheism roughly coincided back around 1500 BC. Monotheism fostered the evolutionary development of our Ego. It was a one-to-one psychological relationship—one Almighty "God" relating to one, consolidating Ego, and repress the polycentric soul, and claim that some abstract soul only comes to importance in the Afterlife. Now everyone would probably agree that our Ego was definitely an important evolutionary development. Actually, we had no choice in this; choice, of course, implies an already emergent Ego able to make choices. However, where then are we today? The Ego has been fully developed, so much so, that our society is utterly Ego-centered, Ego-obsessed, to the point of an Ego dominating narcissism across the culture. The implication for a visionary? The New Age evolutionary development is the transformation of the Ego. Not denying the Ego and its evolutionary purpose, but spiritually transforming it. Implying at the same time liberating our naturally polycentric soul.

The poet is one who names the Gods (Heidegger). So with the guidance of Psyche, I have named our contemporary worldly Gods: Technos (our God of technology), Nihil (our God of nihilism), Ikill (our God of killing and war), Moolah (our God of money and all things related to money), Pow-ER (our God of exercising power, especially over others, especially on the global scene), Ego (our own personal "I" God, the little god we are, of obsessive, narcissistic, self-centered Me Me Me). And I have named in Her revival Aphrodite (our Goddess of love, beauty, and the arts). Are these all of our Gods today? I would not claim that. Undoubtedly Others will be named by other poets, especially when we consider that Psyche has many names. After all, depth psychologist James Hillman was always referring to the polycentric, polytheistic, nature of our soul. And then David L. Miller wrote a book released in 1974, *The New Polytheism*.

Little did I realize when I was setting out to confront the worldly Gods we live with, all the dread and range of overwhelming feelings that would come up. This is one implication of being in the process of Mythos. This is not mental Logos when you can abstractly talk at a distance about different power players and conditions in our world. No, we are talking about Powers active in our Human Unevolved Darkness and bringing those Powers to light...into spiritual Light. These are Powers that could set out to destroy you. Or should I be more global and say, these are Powers that would set out to destroy the world? Certainly Ikill with the technology of Technos could easily destroy humanity with nuclear weapons. And Technos? How many are paying attention to what some in the tech world are saying about AI?

* * *

After the laws of physics, everything else is opinion.
Neil deGrasse Tyson

Though one might pass that off as mere hyperbole, such a statement is actually toxic in collective consciousness.

According to science...

According to science, there is no evidence.
According to science, there is no proof.
According to science, it is not possible.

I am tired of hearing this "According to science..."
I am tired of those invoking science as the arbiter of what is
    possible, of what is real, of what we can experience with
    our own eyes and ears.

I am tired of those invoking science as the bully of what is
and is not.
I am tired of hearing these scientists who are self-proclaimed
experts on Reality.

Can we not pursue science, our love of science, without blinders? Can we not remain awed by the miraculous, the unexplained, to Mystery, to that which is not yet understood? The forceps of scientific method cannot grasp the incredible wonder of Being like a specimen and force it into a box. Anomalous events, miraculous events, are not repeatable, period. As if we don't know that. Science has therefore no overarching authority over what it cannot repeat and experiment upon and be able to predict. Anecdotal evidence is not science, we hear. That is obvious. Was the claim ever made that anecdotal evidence was of the standard of science? If it cannot be predictably held in place by scientific method, again and again, it cannot be captured by science. That certainly does not make the evidence available any less real. That does not make our experience any less real. And it does not deny the fact that such experiences can nonetheless be researched and studied, in another way. For example, the whole phenomenon of UFOs and ETs.

Science is no authority regarding our direct, firsthand experience of gnosis. Science is no authority on Revelation. This is where we must engage Mythos.

Facts

I want only the facts, you say.
You see, facts are scientific, and we today are believers
in science.
Even the management of statistics
& people is a science, involving facts.
We pick facts off a tree called science.
Yes, they are just hanging there like ripe fruit for the picking.
Oh, really?
But who determines the facts…
& what, in fact, is a fact?

What framework of interpretation determines that this
    is a fact?
Is it our Logos tradition that determines this, & only this,
    is a fact?
That determines this, & only this, is science?
Who has authority to say, This, & not that, is a fact?
But, then, how are facts themselves
to be interpreted in the larger cultural context?
What of the facts that are said to be
the correct, mainstream narrative of events?
Are they to be interpreted only by those
who have power? By the Establishment?
By those who get to write the mainstream narratives?
By those who have the money, who provide the funding?
Those who determine the facts are funded by whom?
Who funds the research & the public announcements?
Scientists themselves do not fund
their own research, but depend on universities,
industry, government, grant money.
Might there be a certain vested interest in the research?
Might facts be fudged…slightly fudged?
Might facts be slanted…doctored?
Might facts become a political football?
Can facts be politicized?
Which party gets to own the facts?

Are facts alone nourishment for the soul?
Oh, but according to science, the fact-producer,
so-called soul is not a fact—there is
nothing factual about it, i.e. it does not exist.

September 20, 2020

* * *

Only the Facts

You say you want only the facts & nothing
    but the facts. Okay.
So will facts be the answer to your existence?
Are facts now the meaning of life?
Will facts improve your life?
Will facts drive you to be more creative?
Do facts inspire your soul to develop its native potential?
Do facts replace beauty?
Do facts help you to understand philosophy?
Do facts now take the place of philosophy?
Facts might come into play to help explain ideas
& complex issues, but do they alone explain anything?
Do facts themselves know how to decide what is a fact?
Do facts themselves know how to interpret "the facts"?

Perhaps you should write a book composed of facts.
What kind of facts? That's a good question.
There are dozens of kinds of facts.
How many pages would that book be? Five hundred?
A thousand? Ten thousand? A hundred thousand?
As it's been said, we are awash in facts.
So what will you do with all those facts?

June 12, 2021

* * *

We are told that we now live in the digital age. Everything on the Internet, digital. Almost all our communications, digital. If you use a smartphone, it's digital. All services…banking, medical, our power grid, digital. Everything is data. Yuvah Noah Harrari in his book *Homo Deus* suggests that our new religion is appearing to be Dataism. I find that, however excellent and informative his book is, he comes across as an apologist for Technos and its soon take-over of society as AI.

* * *

Early thoughts on a possible depopulation agenda

One of our culture's biggest taboos for open public conversation is population, or, more accurately, the question if whether Earth might be overpopulated, and who would determine that. Because we are now beginning to hear rumors of a secret elite depopulation agenda. Now to discount population as a relevant topic to address and say that there is actually plenty enough food and resources for everyone living today on the planet then opens to issues of politics, ideologies, the Establishment, the mainstream Status Quo, the System, world banking, the agendas of various elites of wealth and power, even a secret elite that would want to rule over us all. Given these qualifying parameters of power players and an Establishment, a Status Quo, a System, that appears to be rigidly set in place, is there then truly enough for everyone on the planet? Ideally, you would think there should be. R. Buckminster Fuller said as much.

Dennis Meadows, speaking for the globalist Club of Rome, is quoted as saying that the Earth, now holding 7+ billion people, is having to sustain 6 billion too many. Certain globalists apparently see one billion as optimal, meaning that 6 billion people would somehow need to be eliminated. Rumor—"conspiracy theory"—has it that they intend to do this "peacefully" over time through some form of mass euthanasia.

Now if a global elite, with an ear to what the science community, especially the climate science community, has been warning is coming our way, came to the view that Earth has reached its carrying capacity regarding humanity and that something must be done, i.e. depopulating the planet, the question first comes up: Would this view be made public? Of course not. There would be public outrage at such a suggestion. Any depopulation program would have to be clandestine, never mentioned. And so, again, how might it be carried out?

Why go into this dark subject? Because this is a subject that I feel is beginning to fester in the Unconscious of the collective. There is no proving it though

121

at this time. It is the feeling one gets. There are warnings by scientists that humanity cannot go on like this, consuming Earth's resources, and constantly polluting. Now one could say, this has nothing to do with population, the actual problem is the fossil fuel industry, uncontrolled pollution, excessive use of resources, deforestation, etc. that is damaging the planet. It can all be resolved politically, that is, given the correct politics, which will probably never happen. There is also the view that technology will save us; there are plenty of resources, plenty of food, for everyone. But—but—is this how the global elite think about this? Is the global elite only obsessed with their wealth and power? Perhaps there is a group that doesn't think in terms of everyone on the planet eventually living happily together and that technology will come to the rescue. Perhaps they think that population is indeed the problem. Yes, the above-mentioned issues are problems too, but it is increasing population that drives them. What then? Then there are the Transhumanists who envision that they will oversee a diminished, merely biological human population.

Truly, this is dark thinking, you say. I am one, however, who is not afraid to go deep into the Unconscious, into Human Unevolved Darkness, so as to confront the evil within us. I am learning to think how a global elite might think who have unlimited wealth and power. I am learning to think how evil might plot and conspire. Of course, one could shrug this off and say the global elite harbor no such thoughts of depopulation and wouldn't think of conspiring with any such agenda...and besides, there is no unified global elite anyway. The elite who have wealth and power are not that unified, but contend among themselves, as we find at all levels of society. So, then, are there those who are privy to how the global elite might think...again, if there is such a group?

During the Covid pandemic years of 2020-2022, we heard much touted of the Great Reset, but it was not actually explained much in the mainstream. It was primarily promoted by the World Economic Forum (WEF), whose director is Karl Schwab, which began in 1971. It was proposed that the world's economy, conveniently tying in a pandemic (which apparently had previously been anticipated) and a questionable world vaccine agenda, was due for a reset, with implications that the global elite controllers, primarily the G20,

WEF, World Health Organization (WHO), and the World Bank, would come to dominate societal norms more, and would have a greater grip on people's lives. There were rumors that the Great Reset hid a depopulation agenda.

Of course, this kind of thinking is nothing new to perhaps dozens of novelists out there. Let alone, look at so many movies. As it has probably already been said, many of our movies have, in their own way, movie by movie, been conditioning the public to a possible dystopian future...

The belief in an all-seeing "God" seems to keep many people in check. But once the belief in "God" is no longer effective, then human beings have free rein, as it were, especially those who have access to enormous wealth and who have worldly power to carry on agendas behind the scenes. The will to power is therefore free to express itself in whatever way it chooses, having no higher overseer in a "God." Now it is quite possible that a global Postmodern elite has come to this view, that "God" is dead, therefore no "God" is watching over what we do, with a threat of Judgment Day, and that humans are indeed on their own. They are free to create mischief...we could say more strongly, free to do evil on the planet. Let us say, they might have come to the view that Earth has reached its population limit. People cannot keep reproducing with no consequences to the planet. So, then, what are their options? War? Wars are costly and messy, with opposing factions and nations keeping the aggressor at bay; and they don't really depopulate enough. Of course nuclear war would be catastrophic for everyone. And as I've said, war is insanity. But there are all manner of new technologies available today...

* * *

Thoughts on Religions

First, one thing that should be kept in mind is that traditionally religions, yes, are Mythos, but Mythos often traditionally in the Form of extending social control over human behavior. Control of everyday behavior, emotional behavior, moral behavior, sexual behavior, over everyday practices, what we are allowed to express and share, what we are even allowed to think. Consider the repression in Islamic countries still today. Especially, too, when a religion breaks into sects that become cults. Even in Hinduism and Buddhism/Zen there are strict practices to follow…one can be asked to leave from an ashram or monastery if one does not abide by what the guru or master says. In just about every religion, when considered as "control systems," (well-known UFO researcher Jacques Vallee said as much) there has been the historical repression of the full potential of our soul…our psyche.

Christianity

Does Christianity care about our stewardship of Earth? We might hear some lip service. But does Christianity even understand our soul's interconnectedness with Earth? Does Christianity really care about psyche, aka our soul, which it had repressed for 2,000 years? Though we cannot ignore the good charity work that Christians and Catholics do around the world, what is actually the bottom line of Christianity? The Afterlife. The focus has always been on saving the soul, thereby repressing our here and now soul, for the Afterlife. Yes, we hear about some abstract metaphysical "soul." And as if we knew what the Afterlife really entails! (Robert Monroe, famous for his documented/published out-of-body experiences, probably had more to say about the soul outside of our human bubble than the Christian abstraction of soul.) Now if Christianity were to take concern for Earth seriously, it would mean ending for one the Piscean Age dualism between Heaven and Earth. Of course, once we realize—after all, it's taken over one hundred years for Nietzsche's announcement to still be heard—that the old Father Almighty Creator of all the enormously vast Universe is dead, what does Christianity easily collapse into—Postmodern nihilism. (The Christ archetype is a separate, valid issue.) Unfortunately, when it comes to living in this here and now existential life, Christianity, having turned soul into an abstract metaphysical "something," seems unable to confront in any creative way our techno-materialistic world. It's become just another religion one can choose on the Postmodern smorgasbord.

Buddhism

Now why would I be a Buddhist? Why would I want to be, what, ultimately a nihilist? Probably most Westerners who get into Buddhism because it seems to be the hippest religious thing to do don't realize its end game—nothing. All human life, all pursuits, endeavors, all culture, all striving, really come to mean nothing, zilch, zero. Life is ultimately an illusion—or does a Buddhist prefers to put it, life really has no ultimate meaning. The universe has no ultimate meaning…and there is no Divinity, not really. We are all just swimming in an ocean of energy; what we call material reality is just an illusion. Another way to put it: everything just is. So there's no need to strive for anything. Just Be. Here. Now. In this illusion, as is. The Buddhist looks over to his neighbor the Hindu and says, I've checkmated your God Atman—sure, there are higher levels of consciousness, and there are other beings, from demons to various Gods, even your highest of high Atman, or is it Brahmin?—but you must realize it is all an illusion…all these higher states ultimately mean nothing.

This is not to say that meditation doesn't have its benefits. Many of us have practiced meditation to some extent or another. (And there are various Buddhist schools.) We know all about the need to calm the mind and body, to be mindful of all that we happen to be immersed in. It is best to tame desires that get us into trouble, or desires that will never be fulfilled—it is best to let them run dry. Yes, practices that teach letting go of suffering are definitely commendable. Buddhism is valued for its compassionate stance toward others. Buddhism is a good coping religion, better than Christianity in this regard. It is a heuristic religion, a long-term aspirin, a tranquilizer, for the soul. Did I say "soul"? No such thing. Only a convenient umbrella word for this seething cauldron of desires, needs, wants, yearnings, sufferings—a cauldron that's constantly churning about, like Nature…and like Nature, it's all only constant change, change, change—the endless turning kaleidoscope of Being.

To reach this point with Buddhism where all is only an indifferent, universal energy is an exhilarating insight, it is remarkably liberating…but that this would be an existential stance for us to take living in society is asking for the impossible. It is no wonder that one becomes, when Buddhism is taken to this extreme, a Buddhist monk, retiring from the world. And no wonder that Buddhism conveys no strong creative force, which implies being passionate, obsessive, about one's creative work. Has the Dalai Lama, for example, brought forth anything at all that is creatively novel into our world? Any new Vision, Revelation, any new Form, into the world? If we are bringing a new Mythos into the world, why turn solely to Buddhism? I am willing to bring up the Beats even on this issue...look at Jack Kerouac's naive embrace of Buddhism in the midst of the Postmodern decadence around him. And how did he end up?

Hinduism

Eastern spirituality has so often been extolled, even idolized, by quite a few Western individuals. To think, however, that you could simply graft what first comes across as their highly abstract spirituality onto Postmodern Western Ego-incestuous, techno-materialism was so often misconceived. Oh, but you needed first to find yourself a guru—and India had a number of them—and you were on your way to sitting at the feet of a master and learn of the higher knowing levels of consciousness. So travel to India! But back in the 1980s you could find that guru right here in America—Rajneesh (later to be known as Osho). He was at the center of a community up in Oregon, Rajneeshpuram. He thought he could appeal to America's privileged by driving through his fully functioning community, which was totally dedicated to him, in his collection of Rolls Royces? Wearing gold and diamond-studded watches? That was a fundamental social-cultural error of Rajneesh. (But certainly the Eighties decade was known for flaunting one's success and one's wealth.) Was this his clever strategy? (We are not going to let his story go...further commentary will be pursued elsewhere.) We have to admit, he did know his Eastern teachings quite well, though. But his thousands of followers (Rajneeshees), after all these years, what have they done with his teachings? Now of course there were other gurus to choose from...

But Hinduism—its so many versions and schools—might in fact offer the most towards a New Age religious Revelation of Higher/Divine Self. Too, its multitude of Gods speaks to our natural polytheistic soul. For Divine Psyche is the Divine Shapeshifter, appearing to us in many divine guises. Divine Psyche is thereby the Divine Androgyne, both God and Goddess.

(And isn't it curious that Aquarius is the sign of androgyny.) Divine Psyche is likely the New Age name for the thousands-of-year-old Hindu Divine Self known as Atman. (Ken Wilbur made the most of Atman in his book *The Atman Project*.) We could also say that the meditation practice on the Ishta-deva is very much a meditation on Divine Psyche.

Islam

The most regressive, repressive, stagnant world religion, as if still stuck back in the Middle Ages, in the world today would have to be Islam. Islam is the other significant religion to emerge out of the Piscean Age. It translates as "I surrender" / "I submit" to Allah, another monotheistic God. Now look at the Islamic societies still today (though we must consider that various Muslim countries do have some differences). Serious behavior conformity of what is allowed in their culture; strict daily ritual practices; dare not question *The Koran*; freedom of speech and expression limited by Islamic law. Of course, serious repression of women, period, having to wear complete face veils or head scarves. Look at what has happened in Taliban Afghanistan once the United States pulled out. Not following the rigid practices can bring about punishments…even common crimes can bring about horrendous punishments. Islamic countries resist, censor, Western Postmodern culture, yet fully embrace the Western goods of Technos. Most Islamic countries are fully up to date with high-tech cybertechnologies. Saudi Arabia with a fleet of American fighter jets and a replete military arsenal. Iran now with its drone technology, its navy, its nuclear power, and its threatening attempt at developing nuclear weapons. They love Western technology but abhor Western culture.

Islam is perhaps unique in that it is the one major religion born of channeling. Mohammed, uneducated, reputedly not even able to write, heard the channeled inspirations of Angel Gabriel. He is considered the last prophet; Islam has not been and is not open to any other. Though channeling may not be the word Muslims would prefer to hear, in our contemporary context, what else can we call it?

Yet, we cannot ignore the bright spot in Islam known as Sufism. There is much to value in Sufi wisdom and culture. The creative, visionary imagination of Ibn Arabī is superb. So many do admire the poetry of Rumi and Hafiz.

Judaism

Judaism has to be considered the most self-centered of religions. You weren't born a Jew? Well, too bad. The most extreme of them in this regard are called Zionists. You see, *We are the Chosen People* and this is our land. Yahweh told us that. Well, not exactly that. It's coming out, I read, that Yahweh had conditions involving ethical concerns for other people that had to be met before the Israelites could assume land claims. Yes, they were on the cutting edge of monotheism in the evolution of the Ego (however not quite the first regarding monotheism per se). Zionism, of course, takes their chosen relationship to "God" and what they claim is theirs to a self-appointed extreme. This is not to say that *The Old Testament* isn't a remarkable book. It is. It is readable, unlike *The Koran*, filled with riveting stories, miraculous events, poetry, Revelations received by various prophets. Jewish mystics developed the complex, symbolic system of the Kabbalah, its rich symbolism of The Tree of Life, the spiritual writings collected as *Zohar*…all of which can be studied for years.

* * *

Firsthand Observations

There are those who might not take firsthand observations by others seriously. Now it is one thing to simply observe something, and then another to share what one has observed as accurately as possible: *This is what I saw.* Implied here first is a straightforward description. Now another could contend, Is this *exactly* what you saw, plain and simple? Yes, there are those who still might question your plain and simple description. But then, of course, there is almost always another level to your observation. You will probably say more than just a plain and simple description. You would likely have an interpretation for what you saw. Now this is where the other can certainly doubt you and question you, especially when you're sharing about something that is considered controversial. Where did you pick up that interpretation? That interpretation is not exactly mainstream accepted. In fact, it is debunked, discredited. Only professional scientists are qualified to interpret what you saw. The scientists have the official word about that. But then, we might ask, Are the scientists themselves strictly impartial about this? Who might they work for? Who do they answer to? What mainstream narrative are they working within? Do they wish to remain credible, no matter how they might have to fudge? Have they ever considered what is a "fact"? Do they ever get that philosophical?

To Discredit

Oh, he/she has been discredited. How many times have we heard that recently? Now it might in fact be the case that someone has done something to bring about their own discredit. We will set that possibility aside though. What we would like to get a better sense of is how discrediting works. Sometimes the discredit is accomplished as easily as with a wave of the hand: I don't like your position, so I discredit you. So this might be simply a personal prejudice. Most often, though, to discredit someone is to say that it is a judgment made by a community of persons, by a particular social / ideological group, or by those answering to the mainstream. A question such as, Does the person deserve to be discredited? is not asked once the decisive discredit label is slapped on. But the question then implies another question, Discredited by whom? Who has authority to discredit this person? What ideological group discredited this person? Has the person been uniformly discredited by all or by certain vested interests? Is it some power hierarchy that owns the cultural credit system in a society in which it is entitled to pass judgment?

A common ploy is to say the person is discredited by science. Now that might be the case when claims are made that are clearly contrary to accepted scientific fact, when such fact is actually established and demonstrated to be applicable and not just offhandedly assumed. But we know that science per se is not a neutral arbiter of truth, especially regarding controversial topics. Some topics are so complex, or so vague in definitions, or so slippery or unavailable to scientific method, that to invoke science as having made judgment about them violates the notion of an open mind, which should be a prerequisite for beginning scientific inquiry to begin with. We know that science can be rolled out for political purposes.

We live in a system of collective meaning, which confers credit to those who abide by certain accepted meanings. To have credit in society means that you have value, that you have credit with us, because we can count on your experience, views, knowledge, expertise. Your expertise is accredited. And yet, to have such credit doesn't necessarily transfer to the fact of one having credentials per se, however. Credentials (of some kind) are essential in areas of expertise, but they are not any guarantee. One can have credentials and still be discredited for not toting the official, mainstream view on something, for not accepting the official narrative. The official narrative is what confers one's social credit. There is a system of generally accepted narrative meaning and not to abide by it signals that one's credit is now in the category of *dis*—we are now keeping you away from, apart from, out of, our credit system. To discredit that person then means to dismiss that person as having any value in the collective; that person is now in *dis*favor. We are now keeping you away from, apart from, us. It gives one the right then to disrespect, reject, repudiate, that person, and perhaps, even more, to call them names. Without value, the person can now be marginalized, ignored, isolated…that person is persona non grata. To aggressively discredit someone is to symbolically kill that person in the culture.
June 2020

"Wrong"

You are slammed simply with the word 'Wrong,' as in someone more explicitly saying, "You're wrong!" That is the implication. You are wrong, period. But apparently the person doesn't have to exactly spell it out, explain how you are wrong. A person can simply say "Wrong," to something you've spent some time elaborating in writing. The word 'Wrong' seemed sufficient enough. It is assumed you should be satisfied with that. No explanation. Got it? You're wrong! But wrong in what way? What specifically am I wrong about? That one says "Wrong" doesn't say much, does it. Of course, you can ask for an explanation, and there is, yes, a chance you might get one. That is appreciated. Count yourself lucky.

* * *

I was challenged by a friend, When you figure out the meaning of life, please let us know. Well, I have: This is actually quite straightforward, no mystery, no religion: Find your Path and live it consciously and passionately. Yet, a whole essay, a whole lecture, would need to explicate what sounds so straightforward here. And is this much different than what Nietzsche, Jung, Joseph Campbell, Alan Watts, and dozens of others, would essentially say?

How many know what true Passion for their Path in life is? But one must first come to the realization: I know what my Path in life is. It is also called one's destiny.

The Hopi elders have told us that this is no longer a time to be a lone wolf. And yet, the visionary individual is so often marginalized, isolated, forced to live as an outsider…a lone wolf, howling in our Postmodern wasteland.

Are we in the early days of a possible Renaissance in culture? Just look around you. Yes, the world is in crisis. But that is the nature of a transition between Ages. At the same time, it is a Call for visionary Renaissance figures. You have just to courageously stand at The Edge…the Call to new creativity—to be super-creative—is coming through louder and clearer.

Those of us who dare to be the visionaries of today often find that we have an inability to talk fully about our process in a social context, especially in social media. It is so often limited to abstract chitchat. One would think we would have the freedom to talk about our spirituality, at least among those we know, but that is not always the case.

If one can see this Vision of a New Age for oneself, it is an unbelievably powerful inspiration. Alas, artists today, by and large, have so far utterly missed the tremendous potential of this Vision. Most have not finished with the Postmodern, which had its highpoint in the 1980s yet is still the dominant sensibility. I find that so many artists continue to flounder about in Postmodern nihilism and disorientation. How many artists today are inspired by a Vision?

There are those who get so caught up in studies of past traditions that they cannot see and take seriously a new Vision that is shared with them. They keep focusing on the past and fail to see that a new Vision is coming up on the horizon.

Artists, poets, writers are almost always lone wolves. And they are not the only ones. When I've put out the invitation to others for collaboration with *The Mythos*, I get no reply. However, the best example of artists who do know how to collaborate are musicians. Why yes, of course, think of any band, famous or otherwise. Musicians indeed know how to come together to form a band, to play to audiences as a band, and to work together to produce their music for wider and larger audiences. And some bands have played together for years, if not decades. I personally know something of that willingness to collaborate when for about two years I was the poet in a poetry music group going by the name of *Psi Process*.

Today, unless you have made yourself well-known in some way, perhaps even as a celebrity, you can be easily ignored, not taken seriously. You have not yet made it on the cultural radar.

When there are still questions to ask, when there are still questions that go unanswered, one cannot say that truth about a matter is a closed book. But then, perhaps, "truth" about any matter can remain open-ended.

There are those of us today who should take inspiration from the ancient Indian Forest Philosophers who set out to experience all aspects of being human for themselves and then articulated their discoveries in the Vedas. Isn't that what we must be doing today?

I have become a master of patience. How many in this day of constant distractions, constant bustle, constant having to get somewhere, know what patience is?

That others have to suffer hurts me to no end. That is my suffering. But at the same time, I have learned to turn it into compassion.

I wouldn't even have time to indulge in despair. As long as one holds a Vision, there is simply too much work to do, as you must continue on the Path of your Vision.

I didn't know you were on a spiritual Path. Which one? Buddhist? Zen? Vedanta? Do you have a guru? Or is it Christian? The Kabbalah? Sufi? Mystery school? Though I have learned from all of these Traditions, I must say, none of the above. I am on the Path of new Divinity coming-into the world—new Divinity revealed as *The Mythos*: The Story of our Divinity coming-into Human Reality…Psyche.

Now someone wants to talk with me about old traditional notions of "God," the Almighty Father in some abstract Heaven, Creator of the entire Universe (but why quantum reality for that matter), who is said to have created us and who supposedly cares for us. Oh really, watching humanity killing each other en masse in wars, watching atomic bombs dropped on two Japanese cities. (Now "God" as an alias for the mystical experience of Being is another matter.) Well, then, the person is likely talking without realizing it about an Other Intelligence ET. Indeed, to ancient peoples a super-human, super-technological ET easily coming and going in our skies, materializing and dematerializing, could have easily masqueraded as the super-intelligent Creator of all the Universe. Could early humanity have known any better witnessing such super-human magic?

I am certainly not the first one to say this—our culture has elevated materialism as the meaning of life…and more specifically, techno-materialism. This is another way of saying our culture thrives on nihilism. Yes, even as we are entering a New Age.

Have I ever once heard any politician use the word 'Spirit' or the word 'psyche'? Another hint of our schizoid society.

The techno world: that's where the money is, that's where the new power is, that's where the God Pow-ER is epitomized. It is of course also the supreme domain of the God Technos, soon to be the threat of the potential God AI.

An example of our schizoid culture: On the CNN website, a headline news article about a mass shooting with people killed and just above it is placed an ad.

There are those who want to play gatekeepers to us of society's mainstream. They will want to censor and restrict our serious questioning and well thought out criticism of the mainstream Status Quo, especially when mainstream propaganda issued by government and its agencies affects our freedoms and the rightful living of our life. And this is not just us mouthing opinions.

Seems the only way for some of us to keep sane in this Postmodern time we live in is to develop what I call polyphrenia: to be able to be of many minds. Another way to put it is to say, I have a multidimensional Self. But then, isn't this how Psyche appears, what Psyche teaches—Psyche the Divine Shapeshifter, bringing Spirit into all aspects, to the full range of expressions, of our psyche? I envision that more over time will come to realize their polyphrenia.

Those who have had their metaphysical insights, their glimpses of a Higher Self, their paranormal experiences, their Kundalini experiences, their visions, their dreams of launching into greater possibilities with others, but then don't know where to go with them, what to do with them, how to integrate them into daily life. That's where the art of Mythos will eventually come into play.

So much bombards us in this society, coming at us from all directions...all the thousand and one distractions...daily news, sports, politics, 200+ TV channels, surfing the Internet, YouTube videos, new music, new movies, new techie stuff, celebrities to keep up on, bad climate updates, science updates, and now AI is entering society in a big way...so many feel themselves scattered out or numb out...

We live in a society where people simply let the mainstream determine the culture—it thereby becomes the dominant culture. The especially creative, visionary individuals (who are by and large not players in the mainstream) are then left, as they say, creating their own "personal mythology"—developing their own symbols, special words, images—marginalized by the dominant culture. Instead of having the opportunity of contributing to the greater culture, their efforts have no or little impact. That is why scarcely anyone yet understands that Mythos must eventually become a collective Form.

What we find is that people in general, even educated individuals, are basically content with referring to various abstract ideas…spouting abstract ideas, spouting opinions filled with abstractions. Especially when a conversation ventures into metaphysical and spiritual territory. It is the nature of our going culture. And so often it can get confusing, unclear, what exactly they are talking about when we want to get more concrete.

Among many of those we know, we cannot help but have observed this: How many of them in their younger years, their 20s and 30s especially, studied some spiritual teachings, got into Eastern religions, got into meditation, were a member of, or were active in, some metaphysical or spiritual group, had perhaps followed some guru, went on some spiritual pilgrimage, perhaps visited ancient, sacred sites, but then today, where are they? Did they find their Path in life? What happened to all those teachings in their life? What happened to that promise of self-transformation? Why is their psyche now so mainstream Ego-oriented? Why are they so caught up in the contemporary mainstream and its distractions? Didn't any of those earlier years of openness to a Greater Reality perspective have any lasting impact?

There is now and then persons who think that because they have seen a few snippets of our work—and I am referring especially to social media Facebook—that they have a good enough take on what we are about and can therefore make broad, kneejerk judgments about our work, including the outright dismissing our work. Seriously now, for those of us who have multiple works, in a variety of stylistic forms, both published and as yet unpublished, that is sheer presumptuousness. They have no idea of the enormity of what we are about…

All you need is someone—whoever that person might be, whether living or dead, perhaps his or her book(s)—to show you what is possible beyond the everyday boundary of Human Reality and you are inspired to discover new, horizon-expanding possibilities for yourself.

A most dangerous thought, a potentially most crazy-making of thoughts, a thought that the fortress of Ego had supposedly left out, a thought that we assumed had been banished long ago, but a thought that can still to this day be the most inspiring and promising and courageous of thoughts, the thought that can still initiate levering things in a whole other, new direction, is this rather simple, but creatively profound, thought—*that anything is possible.*

In the Sixties, we were familiar with the slogan *Question Authority.* Well, my motto has become *Question the System.* You see, authorities can always shrug their shoulders and say, But I'm only following what the System has been established for.

How is a New Age herald, a New Age prophet, to live in this society? Must he have followers? Must he set himself up as some guru? Must he be on social media and have followers? Must he be a professional of some kind? A professor perhaps? Must he have sufficient money to market himself? Must he at least have a website? Must he produce YouTube videos? To say that he is only an obscure poet, even if a visionary poet, is he condemned then to always live his life precariously at The Edge…a lone wolf?

To advocate for the love of others, for all humanity. I hear this among the spiritually awakened and I, too, am an advocate of a love for all, and in spreading this universal Christ message. But we find that politicians, world leaders, the power and wealthy elite, even most celebrities, are assumed not to be concerned about this universal Christ message; they are considered exempt from speaking of a love for humanity. Think about it, those having the most influence do nothing to help spread the universal word of love to others. They think only in terms of the System—power, prestige, wealth, self-aggrandizement.

Collective reality is defined by the mainstream, the market/consumerism, mass media, social media, politics, science, and all current technology…all of this can be considered subsumed under the Establishment, the Status Quo, the System. And there is our personal life, which in the System we live in, unless one is wealthy, has power, or is a celebrity, counts for nil.

There are those who say they have questioned enough. They finally give in to what the government, the mainstream Status Quo, claims as the answers, especially regarding controversial issues or subjects. They've had enough of questions and want to move on.

The mainstream would want you to live and think in narrow, engineered channels that keep you confined within the System. But consider that your life and your thinking can be a mighty river fed by thousands of streams across the culture, a watershed of multitudes of peoples all adding their voices to your river…a living, unrestrainable, liberated river of voices that endlessly finds its way to the great Ocean Universal. The Ocean of freedom, the Ocean of unlimited potential, the Ocean of Vision. I say, Be such a mighty river…

I awoke this morning and immediately thought, Joy! Joy! Joy! that I have another day to be utterly open to encounter Being…and am utterly ready to step this day into its revealed Fountain of Unlimited Creativity, hinting of our own Divinity!

www.ingramcontent.com/pod-product-compliance
Lightning Source LLC
Chambersburg PA
CBHW051629120626
46551CB00014B/2001